Praise for *The 7 Resolutions*

This is the best book I have read that balances a life motivated by grace yet also shows the need for spiritual disciplines. It avoids the errors of legalism and also the opposite errors of permissive grace. Yes, it does show clearly where self-help ends and God's power begins. Karl's honesty and vulnerability about his own struggles makes this book welcoming, and hope filled. It provides specific direction for every one of us who long to see God's continuing transforming power in our lives.

Erwin Lutzer
Pastor Emeritus, The Moody Church, Chicago

Karl Clauson has spent decades helping people as a pastor and radio personality live out their new spiritual life and calling. The message of *The 7 Resolutions* comes from Karl's study of the Word and thousands of conversations with struggling people. I strongly recommend this book to anyone living in the frustrating gap between where you know you should be spiritually and where you currently are at.

Mark Jobe
President, Moody Bible Institute

From time to time a book comes along that offers more than a good story line or helpful insights. It feels anointed. That's my sense of Karl Clauson's *The 7 Resolutions*. It carries prophetic calls we desperately need today to counter the ever-darkening culture now challenging us. Its truth powerfully penetrates the "soft" Christianity and self-effort so many believers are mired in. It's so on-target for our day. I cannot recommend it strongly enough . . . not just to read, but vital truth to gather around with others and master. It's that needed!

Robert Lewis
Pastor, founder of Men's Fraternity and BetterMan

Every one of us has heard the voice of the accuser . . . "you can't," "you won't," "you aren't . . ." As broken people, it's easy to fall prey to his insidious lies about our own failings and to descend into a pit of darkness that surrounds our soul. You can try to claw your way out on your own or you can grab the lifeline of God's strength and His promises. This book is about pulling you out of that darkness—of remembering who God is and what He says about YOU. You can try to fix the issues you are facing on your own, or you can grab on to the One whose power and love can rescue you from any pit. The choice is yours, but this book will help you make the better choice. Read it—and resolve to let God take control.

Janet Parshall
Host / Executive Producer, *In the Market with Janet Parshall*

Karl Clauson is driven by a bold and unshakable faith that you can be free! His confidence in God's power to radically heal you from addiction, pain, and brokenness is not theoretical; it comes from his own personal healing journey and encounter with God's liberating grace. *The 7 Resolutions* is a clarion call to anyone who is ready to join God and kill sin! In Christ . . . freedom starts today!

Chris Brooks
Senior Pastor, Woodside Bible Church; host, *Equipped with Chris Brooks*

In his wonderfully practical book, Karl offers deep insight and biblical wisdom for lasting change. If you're looking for tools to defeat the lies in your mind and overcome negative patterns of thinking, run and get this book.

LINA ABUJAMRA
Author of *Fractured Faith*; founder, Living with Power Ministries

When Karl speaks or writes, I listen. He is one of the most authentic and inspiring men I know. He will light up your life in one second. I find myself smiling and excited about life every time I'm around him. Karl had me from the first page of this book. God has miraculously changed Karl's life and He wants to do the same with yours. Jump into *The 7 Resolutions* and let God transform you into the person He created you to be!

DAVE WILSON
Host of *Family Life Today*

The Bible says in John 14:26, "But the Helper, the Holy Spirit, whom the Father will send in my name, he will teach you all things and bring to your remembrance all that I have said to you." Karl addresses how that truth can lead his readers to real healing and growth instead of the world's counterfeit. It's refreshing to hear the truth.

BEN CALHOUN
Lead singer and songwriter, Citizen Way

I love this book! Thank you, Karl, for so clearly underscoring the reality that Jesus is in the business of transforming our lives. We can indeed win our biggest battles. But we are not passive bystanders in our victories. *The 7 Resolutions* points to the reality of our part in receiving and experiencing God's promises for our lives: decision and resolve. You will find, however, that these resolutions are not anchored in "bootstrapping" self-determination, leading to failure and frustration. No, they are expressions of our reliance on the power of the Holy Spirit to produce change and transformation. Thank you, my brother, for this treasured gift!

DR. CRAWFORD W. LORITTS JR.
Author, speaker, radio host; founder and President of Beyond Our Generation

The 7 Resolutions resource that you are holding in your hands delivers straight talk from a genuine and authentic man: Karl Clauson. His vulnerable style of writing puts you in the room with him whether you listen to him on radio, sit under his teaching at conferences or church, or walk with him as a friend as I have the honor of doing. This isn't self-help. This is all about joining God and experiencing the real deal of His wisdom, love and grace. Read it. Digest it. Share it. Open your heart to God's truth and promises and put on your seatbelt for the ride of *The 7 Resolutions*.

DR. GARY ROSBERG
America's Family Coaches; author, speaker, marriage coach

The 7 Resolutions is written by a man who has been changed by the power of almighty God. It flows from the heart of a man who longs to see disciple-makers raised up and multiplying. You can feel Karl's passion and his hunger for kingdom advancement on page after page. It's one of those books you can't put down and wish you had read decades sooner! If you thirst for first-century, New Testament, book of Acts Christianity, read the book. You won't regret it!

DAVID NELMS
Founder and President, TTI

THE 7 RESOLUTIONS

WHERE SELF-HELP ENDS AND GOD'S POWER BEGINS

KARL CLAUSON

MOODY PUBLISHERS
CHICAGO

Scripture quotations marked KJV are taken from the King James Version.

All emphasis in Scripture has been added.

Names and details of some stories have been changed to protect the privacy of individuals. Some persons in this book are composites.

Versions of certain sections in this book, including The Time Is Now, The Giants Are Still There, and The Secret were previously published on the author's website at karlclauson.com. Content in the Choose Friends chapter originally appeared on the Moody Radio website (moodyradio.org).

Edited by Amanda Cleary Eastep
Interior design: Puckett Smartt
Cover design: Derek Thornton / Notch Design
Author photo: Claudia Lumperdean

Library of Congress Cataloging-in-Publication Data

Names: Clauson, Karl, author.
Title: The 7 resolutions : where self-help ends and God's power begins / Karl Clauson.
Other titles: The seven resolutions
Description: Chicago : Moody Publishers, 2022. | Includes bibliographical references. | Summary: "Discover the seven agreements you make with God that will overthrow old patterns and bring real change. A new you awaits-a transformation that God wants to do in your life. It won't be easy. It won't happen overnight. But it'll be worth it, because growth beats stagnation every time"-- Provided by publisher.
Identifiers: LCCN 2021037362 (print) | LCCN 2021037363 (ebook) | ISBN 9780802425096 | ISBN 9780802476609 (ebook)
Subjects: LCSH: Spiritual formation. | Change (Psychology)--Religious aspects--Christianity.
Classification: LCC BV4511 .C535 2022 (print) | LCC BV4511 (ebook) | DDC 248.4--dc23
LC record available at https://lccn.loc.gov/2021037362

LC ebook record available at https://lccn.loc.gov/2021037363

Originally delivered by fleets of horse-drawn wagons, the affordable paperbacks from D. L. Moody's publishing house resourced the church and served everyday people. Now, after more than 125 years of publishing and ministry, Moody Publishers' mission remains the same—even if our delivery systems have changed a bit. For more information on other books (and resources) created from a biblical perspective, go to www.moodypublishers.com or write to:

Moody Publishers
820 N. LaSalle Boulevard
Chicago, IL 60610

1 3 5 7 9 10 8 6 4 2

Printed in the United States of America

I dedicate this book to my bride, Junanne. Jubes, you've partnered with me in the gospel with a beautiful faith and unflappable courage. Your genuine love for God is contagious, and your passion for people is sweet. Few know how powerful your influence is—you even got me to love our rescue cats. God's best blessings to you, babe!

CONTENTS

INTRODUCTION

RADICAL CHANGE IS POSSIBLE

The drapes over the windows and doors hung, torn and sagging, like the souls of everyone in the dimly lit home that night. I had never met the man who sat across from me. He stretched out to hand me the clear glass pipe freshly loaded with crystal methamphetamine. I took a hit, and in a moment, the drug's rush was followed quickly by crushing condemnation.

I could touch and taste the evil in that dark room. Demons dropped their disguise and went all out. My mind was being assaulted by cruel and vile words: "You're done, you piece of garbage! Call yourself a Christian, but you know, Karl, what a complete loser you are. Quit pretending to have found God. If people knew the real you, they'd trash you and your weak God."

How God pulled off what happened next, I'll never fully understand. He gave me the strength to bolt from that place. As I ran through the room, I didn't know if I'd get tackled or shot. At this point, I didn't care; I just had to get out of there. When I crashed through the front door, I was running for my immediate safety but really I was trying to outrun my shame.

That two-mile stretch of road to find some sanity and security was a blur. God was carrying me, but Satan talked my ear off, telling me I was unredeemable and deserved to die. Opening the front door to the place I was staying, I shuffled quietly to my bedroom, falling to my knees. The shame blanketed me. I could barely breathe. I was starting to believe some wars couldn't be won. The predictions of family and friends that I'd never really change were coming true. One last thought dropped in my mind: "There's nothing new about you." Heaving in tears, I asked God to go ahead and kill me.

It was a classic descent into darkness. I had knocked off from work on a Friday after framing the walls of a new health club. It had been a long hot day in central California. Saying yes to getting some cool drinks at a nearby place seemed innocent enough. But for me, I had just ascended a dangerous slide and slipped down its slick, steep surface—this never ended well for me. Predictable stiff drinks followed those cool drinks, and I was primed for whatever would come my way. Within hours I was in one of the darkest places and darkest times of my life.

In all my bottoming out, I had never gone this low. But to do it now was shattering. Just three weeks prior, I was delivered from my prison of self—transformed by the power of God. This shameful night happened *after* the light of Jesus had shined into the darkness of my soul and saved my life.

There was no question that God had changed me before this horrible event. After years of running from God, all while faking it for family and friends who loved me, God asked me, "Are you done yet?" I was so done. I was only twenty-three years old, but I had already exhausted the possibility that alcohol, cocaine, and more workplace acclaim could fill the God-shaped void in my life. In a moment, God changed me. I wept tears of hope. The sun was brighter, the sky bluer—I finally experienced what it meant to be born all over again. My new life was breathtaking.

But there I was, a three-week-old failed follower of Jesus. I had just moved to a new town to get a fresh start and be mentored by my uncle. Now here I was starting to buy the lie that life would never really change for me. Evil was taunting me with this one thought: "You might even be a child of God, but some of your battles just can't be won."

This book is about winning your biggest battles. It's about believing God's promises and resolving to follow His plan for embracing them. It's about overcoming what is defeating you. Becoming a child of God means beating addictions, altering destructive behaviors, and killing bad habits that you've grown accustomed to or possibly written off as unwinnable. It's time to come alive. The 7 Resolutions can serve as your agreement with God to give Him full control and discover that the toughest battles can be won.

Never measure God and His power to change you by your current standard of living. This standard is far more than financial. It's emotional, relational, spiritual, professional—every aspect of life. If you have truly believed that Jesus both died for your sins and came up out of the grave and lives today—and if you have turned around 180 degrees to follow Him—you already know the path you walk has plenty of challenges. But the promises and extravagant abundance of life in Christ are inestimable.

- You have been given access to every spiritual blessing. (Eph. 1:3)
- You are empowered by God to experience the unimaginable. (Eph. 3:20)
- You have received a spirit of power, love, and sound mind. (2 Tim. 1:7)
- You are uniquely designed by God to do great work. (Eph. 2:10)
- You have been chosen and destined to bear much fruit. (John 15:16)
- You are free in Christ and no longer a slave to sin. (Gal. 5:1)
- You are dead to your old life and alive in Christ. (Gal. 2:20)
- You can now be strengthened and matured through trials. (James 1:4)

But a problem has to be addressed: there seems to be a gap (often a big one) between God's promises for Christ followers and what we actually experience in our day-to-day lives. These gaps are too common: God's promised peace vs. our consistent stress; God's promised wisdom for trials vs. our flying blind through life's storms; God's promised victory over destructive habits vs. our hiding those things that are robbing, killing, and destroying us. God wants to close these gaps!

God is never content to let us settle for too little. We sometimes get a taste of what could be, and then we slip back into old patterns of living. God's promises seem just out of reach. Sometimes we settle for too little because we compare ourselves to others and conclude we're not doing that bad. This comparison then holds us in a place of compromise—never taking the higher road and opting for less.

I know the destructive thinking that rattles around in your mind. And I also know what God says about you. I know the brutal battles you fight on that barren land between the bait of Satan and the promises of God. I also know what it feels like faking aspects of your faith, trying and failing to manage your sin, and hiding in your pain and shame—you feel desperate for it to stop right now. But the solution is far bigger than yourself.

A radical shift in thinking may be in order here. The solution has nothing to do with our own strength. "Self-help" is a threat to God's children. The temptation to fight our battles in our strength and not with Holy Spirit power dates back to the Fall. Two thousand years ago, Paul chastised a church for self-help lifestyles: "Are you so foolish? Having begun by the Spirit, are you now being perfected by the flesh?" (Gal. 3:3). We too start off utterly dependent on the Spirit, but for multiple reasons, we shift onto tracks of self-help. The word "flesh" represents all we can muster apart from God's Spirit, and it will never cut it.

People are sinking under the weight of human efforts. The phrase "God helps those who help themselves"[1] has its own Wikipedia page. And by the statistics, it would appear that many of God's kids believe this is probably true. Fifty-two percent of adults who call themselves Christian accept a works-oriented means to God's acceptance. Even more troubling is that seventy percent of Catholics, forty-six percent of Pentecostals, forty-four percent of Protestants, and forty-one percent of evangelicals believe a person can qualify for heaven by being or doing good.[2] Anecdotally, most people I've talked with who believe solidly in *sola fide* (faith alone) don't always live like it's true. They find it all too common to slip into a mindset that their worth is linked to their performance. Self-help is more than spiritual irritation; it's a battle they want to win.

Self-help, as defined by Merriam-Webster, is "the action or process of bettering oneself or overcoming one's problems without the aid of others."[3] Living like this is actually a double whammy. It cuts us off from both God and His children, fellow believers God put in our lives to help us. The dynamic spiritual life is a team sport. Our individual God-given skills, talents, creativity, and ingenuity have been leaned on to a fault and led us to a fabulous dead end. Even though God is calling us to acknowledge Him in all our ways, we are too often leaning on our own understanding (Prov. 3:5–6). We sing about trusting God, but we live like we're trusting self.

This brand of Christianity will only stay the same if we do more of the same. A radical shift must happen. Like a train a switchman guides from one set of tracks to another, we need to be redirected from any attempt at helping ourselves and shifted to experience God's power moment by moment. Living in God's power is the only path forward that doesn't end in exhaustion, tragic compromise, or ruin.

I'm inviting you to an adventure. I want to help you get off the self-help train and ride the winds of God's power. That's why I have written the 7 Resolutions. The 7 Resolutions are seven core disciplines to help you trust God and not rely on your own strength. These disciplines are core because God repeatedly features the value of each in Scripture, from Genesis to Revelation; and the promises attached to each of them are nothing short of breathtaking. These resolutions will provide lasting help to you in areas of your life where you could never help yourself. Although not easy to hear or apply, they are solidly biblical, clearly actionable, and captured in a way to help you fully live in God's power.

WE SING ABOUT TRUSTING GOD, BUT WE LIVE LIKE WE'RE TRUSTING SELF.

This is about getting off the self-help train and redirecting yourself to get aligned with God. Prevailing over the gates of hell and silencing the legions of voices of evil is totally in step with God's purpose for your life. You want it, but in your strength you simply can't get it. God is ready and eager to do with you what you can't do by yourself. You just have to ask.

You're not the only person who wrestles deeply with personal failings and feeling like a spiritual impostor. By God's grace, I'm no longer the man I was in that dark place and time as a new follower of Jesus. The battle that almost caused me to quit now seems like a distant memory. God won the war over cocaine, whiskey, and deadly choices—and to do it, He conquered Satan and my tendency to think victory is up to me. He wants to do the same for you no matter what you battle!

For over twenty years, I've had a personal mission statement for my life that is the WHY for writing this book: "I exist to inspire a spiritual revolution within the church that reaches the world." I'm sold out to my calling and confident of God's power to ignite a spiritual revolution in *your* life. I'm confident you'll see God overthrow those negative forces that have governed and diminished your life.

For most of my adult life, I've enjoyed learning how to take hold of God's promises personally; but the adrenaline rush of helping others experience radical transformation is an equal thrill. I've learned some from my victories, but my most profound learning has been through my failures. Being forced to test God's truth through the highs of sustained spiritual revivals, the slog of common personal sin, and the lows of relational betrayal has been a good teacher. I've had to face my brokenness in the mirror of reality and watch God take me to the end of myself—strategically positioned for life change.

After thirty-five years of frontline ministry, you learn a bit about how people change. Through cross-cultural ministry in Asia and South Africa, leading a thriving church of thousands of people in Alaska, and hearing from some of the two hundred and fifty thousand people who listen weekly to the radio show I've been privileged to host on weekday mornings in Chicago, I've seen what true discipleship looks like and how taking hold of God's promises happens. Being a disciple or follower of Christ is not a name to claim, a class to take, or rules to follow. It's a total and complete surrender of your life to the One who makes all things new. It's courageous, honest, brutal, countercultural, and above all, humble.

God has given me a unique vantage point to watch His power transform individuals and groups of people. I've had the joy of learning what "first steps" to give thousands of new Christ followers who didn't know where to go. Through a handful of young evangelists in remote Talisay, Batangas, Philippines, God taught me more about perseverance and overcoming persecution than I ever could have learned Stateside.

I learned the power of prayer in a thriving single adult ministry in Arkansas. And now I'm seeing the power of unity in a diverse young church in the heart of Chicago whose people prove that clinging to God and each other is beautiful. All these settings have allowed me a high-definition view of truly becoming new, and I believe it will help you.

My bride of thirty-four years, Junanne, had a little project for me at the end of one Christmas season—fix a few broken tree ornaments that had lost their heads and various other parts so we could put them away whole. I placed a drop of glue at the breakpoint and pressed the pieces together. The only question I had was: Would it hold? After the prescribed time, I gave it a bump. It seemed stable, so I twisted a little more firmly. Snap! Wouldn't you know the original fix held firm, but another area of weakness was exposed?

That's your life and mine. We have broken pieces and areas of weakness that God is healing and putting back together. And even though we won't be entirely whole until we cross over to the other side, God wants to redeem, restore, and revitalize the ugliest and most broken parts of us. I'm so confident that God can overhaul the most demanding challenges, habitual failings, and your deepest pains that I don't want you to focus on a rather small flaw in your life. Go big! Give God something that's broken. Give Him the hidden mess, the worst parts of you. Put truth to the test.

Change is possible. Watch God overthrow what has been broken for years with seven resolutions that will launch your life into a new spiritual orbit. Believe God to do what you haven't been able to achieve through your best efforts. Come out of the shadows of shame, and trust God to heal what has been hidden. Give God the ugliest, most unseemly, and shattered pieces of your life. You know you can't fix it, and He's up to the challenge.

Chapter 1

WRECKED

Failure is not fatal, but failure to change might be.[1]

John Wooden

I don't love you anymore." With five simple words and a quivering chin, Junanne told me how far our marriage had fallen. There we were with our new home, two little kids, down the path of family life a few years, and waist-deep in a thriving ministry. At that moment, my world caved in.

I was wrecked. My whole life to that day had been about achievement. Adventure, competitions, rescues, extreme work environments—I had faced all of these and succeeded at most. But now I had no answers. The man who thought he could win it, build it, or fix it had nothing to say. As I walked away from Junanne into the bathroom, everything inside me wanted to cover my shame with blame—rattling off her sins and how she had failed me. She certainly had them, and she would have graciously owned up to each one. But God had a meeting scheduled with me. I needed to come face-to-face with the fact that I had failed to be the man God called me to be and that Junanne deserved.

As I stared at myself in the mirror, I was faced with a big decision. Would I allow my mind to dwell on the shortcomings of my wife, or would I face who I was and own my contributions to the loveless marriage my bride felt shackled to? It was a "come to Jesus" moment. God was brutally merciful and gave me a peek at my soul, and it wasn't pretty.

I had completely neglected my promise to love my bride as Christ loves the church. By strength of personality, I had rationalized my inaction and minimized what she felt. Ministry momentum and growing numbers of young Jesus followers became an excuse for distraction and my work addiction. I had spiritualized the pace of my life, and she was even buying what I was selling for a good long stretch. I had pushed Junanne into a forced fast in our marriage—I was starving her from love. God began to break me and shine the light on my brokenness. Through my tears, I could see God was up to something.

As much as her words felt like the end, it was just the beginning of something extraordinary. Junanne had just given us a chance at love. Real love. Intimate love. Honest, warm, knowing love. Love that hangs out the truth without fear and confidence that God can fix what's broken. No longer did we have to live as glorified roommates who shared a couple of kids, groceries, common enemies, yearly vacations, and occasional sex.

With those five words and that quivering chin, God shattered the façade of a dynamite marriage. Now the reality of what I had built was exposed for me to see. We had mastered the art of sharing what we *thought* (usually cruel digs) about each other, yet never getting down to what we *felt* about each other. We had learned to build up protective walls, and exchanging important information was as intimate as it got. What was dysfunctional felt normal, acceptable, and sadly, better than most other relationships.

I had helped build a marriage system that kept us looking pretty good on Sundays. We weren't shaking a fist at God and rejecting His plan; we had just settled for too little and learned how to survive it. We had our moments of laughter and fun. And our love for our son and daughter gave us the resolve we needed to stay together. Divorce was never an option, but what we had was so short of God's best. This moment in the mirror led to an awakening in our marriage—God wanted me to be a man who initiated and took the lead in acts of love. God was about to show me whole new patterns of living. The power of really listening was an art class God put me in, and He re-enrolls me every year. God showed me that He could breathe life into dead things, even a dead marriage. He also showed me something fun—chivalry still got style points from my wife.

The next few months brought on some dramatic changes. God kept the mirror of my failure in front of me. He loved us enough to allow me to sit with my pain. Amazingly, God began to reward my posture of brokenness with His power to love Junanne as she deserved. God placed a passion within me to be a good husband. I carved out time in my day planner to date the girl I loved. We began to talk and listen to each other to the point where we each *felt* heard and valued. If I told you it was an easy or quick fix, that would be a lie.

The constant risk of falling into the ditch of apathy was and is a present danger. But radical change can happen. Grace is more than a word—God has the power to do in us what we can't do ourselves.

After thirty-four years of marriage, I can say with joy, Junanne is my best friend.

GOD CAN FIX THAT

If you're normal, you have a secret fear that some of the broken stuff in your life will never get repaired and that some of your dreams simply won't be realized. Suspicions that "God's promises will never be fully experienced," "that addiction is unwinnable," and "those patterns will never be fully broken," are like a family secret that everyone knows, but no one talks about. Well, let's bring that lie into the light of truth. God has this way of illuminating our broken pieces so nothing is hidden and, at the same time, cleaning and fixing us up without condemnation.

> **"WHAT ARE THE DESTRUCTIVE PATTERNS OR BROKEN SYSTEMS IN MY LIFE THAT KEEP ME CONFINED TO A LIFE I DON'T WANT TO LIVE?"**

Please don't shy away from the truth. See it, own it, and believe that God can fix it. But be alert to this: some truths about God have been twisted and destroyed. Let's reclaim it right now. Word on the street is that God approves of religious performers and condemns sinners. It's exactly the opposite! The life of Jesus shows the true character of God—He condemned the self-righteous performers and saved sinners. Never be afraid of the light of Jesus; He's here to help those of us who are willing to admit our need.

When taking stock of how you're failing and where you're headed in any area of your life, one question is paramount. It's not the question of what life you want to live. The question is this: "What are the destructive patterns or broken systems in my life that keep me confined to a life I don't want to live?" These patterns and systems have consequences. There is no way you can pull yourself up to reach God's promises. Bootstrapping won't cut it. Grit is good for the short haul but fails with the slightest whiff of weariness or discouragement. I've started many goals with a flurry and had huge start-up success, only to be crushed with the weight of my failure and feelings of being caught in a cage I could never escape.

It's easy to believe that our failures will forever define us and that God is disgusted with us. We even question God's ability to overcome our inability. Seemingly unable to get a grip on life, we fake it, give up, or settle for a life that we consider "better than most." If this describes you, stay calm. You haven't lost your mind or your salvation. You need a revolution of your inner being. A total overthrow of the systems that ultimately govern and direct the life you live.

BROKEN SYSTEMS

No one is around, the music fades, and life punches you in the face. That's the best time to measure how your systems for living life are working for you. There is a gap between our desire to live powerfully and the reality of living in God's grace and power. Systems exist in this gap—spiritual, emotional, and relational. By systems, I mean behavioral patterns that—whether good, bad, or ugly—shape us, guide us, and produce outcomes consistent with the system.

Some systems are clearly visible; many are internal systems that can't be seen by others but negatively impact our lives. Systems formed out of sin, insecurity, discouragement, destructive traditions, family dysfunction, rebellion, pride, and other toxic sources are simply broken. We either invented these systems for survival, adopted them from peer groups, or inherited them from family. Some live isolated lives because a vulnerable confession was thrown back in their face. Others are habitually critical because that's just how their friends roll. And still others have been trained by parents to look down at anyone who doesn't look like them. Broken systems are myriad, and they manifest themselves in any number of destructive ways.

All the desire and our best human effort can't seem to overcome the gravitational pull of the broken systems that hold us down. Like us kids who tried to fly by wildly flapping our arms, achieving only sheer exhaustion with no liftoff. These hurtful and destructive systems need to be overthrown by God if you're going to experience abundant life and grasp God's promises.

In the Bible, every great example of spiritual victory and conquest over broken systems paints a picture of revolutionary moments.

King David lived in a system of indulgence. Second Samuel chapters 11 and 12 reveal the epic story of David's repentance and restoration. His power and reckless desire for sexual gratification ultimately crushed a young family's dreams, killed innocent lives, and brought massive pain into his own heart. Only through the deep breaking of the system of "self" did David find the breakthrough.

God's grace and Jesus' ability to expose our sin without shaming our soul is on full display in John chapter 4. The nameless woman at a water well with Jesus lived in a system of shame and isolation. Everything about her was "lesser than." Her people, the Samaritans, were considered dogs by the Jewish elite. Her life choices left her shacked up with a man after five failed marriages—her life was a mess. Being exposed but not rejected by Jesus compelled her to share her freedom story. Through her life, God's power caught fire in the community and led to a massive liberation in the region.

Want to see how much God hates the broken system of religious performance, living for the approval of others, and checking those boxes? God saves His most scathing words for the pretenders—the Pharisees, Jewish spiritual leaders distinguished by strict observance of the traditional and written law and pursuing superior sanctity. They were respected by many, and some Pharisees were well-intentioned God seekers. But their system of performance and pride missed the mark. They had put God in a box and wanted everyone else to do the same. It was an empty religion, and Jesus called the system for what it was—like a well-used travel mug, reasonably clean on the outside but filthy on the inside. Jesus never waters down truth: "Now you Pharisees cleanse the outside of the cup and of the dish, but inside you are full of greed and wickedness. You fools! Did not he who made the outside make the inside also?" (Luke 11:39–40).

Here's the uncompromising truth: as much as we don't want to admit it, there's a little bit of Pharisee in you and me. I had a caller to my radio show share a statement that stuck with me: "We judge ourselves by our best intentions, but we judge others by a single moment of weakness." Christian, beware and examine your spiritual life thoroughly before trying to help others spiritually!

Of all the broken systems, self-help can be uniquely destructive. Self-help books are in a category on Amazon with approximately 70,000 different titles. I have a few shelves of the best self-help books. Although there are great truths packed into self-help books on topics like discipline, habits, time management, etc., they fail when they put the onus upon us to succeed in our efforts alone. The problem is that for all the writing, reading, blogging, and TED-talking, self-help only produces a small fraction of people who see and experience sustainable wins.

To be fair, God's calling is higher than most self-help enthusiasts are aiming. The gospel goes to the soul of a man or woman. The gospel gets into messes that self-help doesn't even try to address. The gospel intends to alter the direction of our life and the very way we walk through this life. This work is tough, thorough, and impossible if not for God. The most authoritative author of Christian living, other than Jesus, was Paul. And look at how he approached witnessing and disciple making: "For this I toil, struggling with all his energy that he powerfully works within me" (Col. 1:29). Paul wouldn't touch self-help. His life and ministry was all about God's power—and that's what we need!

Paul actually got delivered from self-help and performance-based faith. He said he'd take on anyone if self-help and religious performance was measured, "though I myself have reason for confidence in the flesh also. If anyone else thinks he has reason for confidence in the flesh, I have more" (Phil. 3:4). Any effort outside of God's power got him nowhere! One of the best anecdotal pieces of evidence is the twelve steps of Alcoholics Anonymous. The founders knew that humble submission to God was central to freedom from addiction. Even the modern version of the steps refers to the need for a "higher power." We know this to be God.

Here's the harsh reality about dreams, goals, and ultimately, self-help: only 9.2 percent of people actually achieve the resolutions they aspire to at the beginning of each year.[2]

Hold on here! You should have a question for me right now. Why in the world write a book about seven resolutions if resolutions fail 90.8 percent of the time? Because almost all resolutions are attempted in our own strength! Let me tell you what makes the 7 Resolutions different:

- The 7 Resolutions embrace our weakness and are only achieved in God's power; they position us for more of His presence. (Isa. 40:29)

- The 7 Resolutions don't enable you to reach your dreams, but empower you to join God, who can do exponentially more than you can imagine. (Eph. 3:20–21)

- The 7 Resolutions are expressions of God's grace—engage with them fully, and you'll find increasing strength. (2 Cor. 12:9)

Wise decision-making, parenting victories, relational success, attainment of your professional stride, fiscal responsibility, and even those things beyond imagination are not unreachable. But God gives you the freedom to decide.

This is simply irrefutable: God sent Jesus to save you from your sin and transform your life, defeating destructive systems and getting your life aligned with His. Although not everyone will take hold of God's promises and the precepts that get us there, God has always put the choice before His people. "I have set before you life and death, blessing and curse. Therefore choose life, that you and your offspring may live" (Deut. 30:19). The choice to take hold of it—it's in your court.

Prepare to look within yourself. Take an honest look at the systems that work and those that are broken. While the broken systems need to be shut down, others, like redeeming time, may just need to be aimed at your calling or spiked with spiritual nutrients. It's time to take an honest look at who you really are, see how it's working, agree with God on needed changes, and get moving in "His energy."

IT DOESN'T HOLD WATER

When God's people walked away from Him and tried to carve out a life for themselves, He sent a prophet! Jeremiah was a prophet who didn't hold back. He told the people just what he heard from God. We love to quote Jesus, "The truth will set you free"; but tradition holds that the truth got the prophet Jeremiah stoned to death. It seemed that anytime Jeremiah dared to speak truthfully, he was falsely accused, beaten, imprisoned, or thrown in a cistern and left for dead.

Jeremiah's words might not have gotten him killed today, but for sure, he'd be silenced. He was assessing the emptiness of God's children and made a bold statement:

> "Be appalled, O heavens, at this;
>   be shocked, be utterly desolate,
> declares the LORD,
> for my people have committed two evils:
> they have forsaken me,
>   the fountain of living waters,
> and hewed out cisterns for themselves,
>   broken cisterns that can hold no water."
> (Jer. 2:12–13)

Jeremiah nailed it then, and his words ring true today. We've abandoned the God who wants to fill our lives and dismantle our self-constructed cisterns (systems) that can't hold water. Cisterns were reservoirs carved out of rock that stored fresh water. Here's what we've done. We've built systems for ourselves that can't deliver what we'd hoped or what we need. They leak and come up empty when it comes to God's promises. We need to ask ourselves: What kind of life have I carved out for myself, and does it hold water?

The real test for a cistern would have been a dry season. When the refreshing runoff from the rainy season was over, the grass dying, the river dried up, and the sun beating down—would the cistern still hold water? That's the test for us too. When we enter the desert seasons, we see how we're made and if what fills us will sustain us.

No matter how much God pours into us through various means, we can struggle to find soul satisfaction, oftentimes because parts of us aren't visibly broken but we have leaks. All the apps, online messages, and dynamic worship experiences can't seem to fill us up. And no matter how good our intentions, we're just not growing.

Here are a few examples of broken systems that cause us to leak:

- We lack essential spiritual disciplines, so we miss out on hearing the voice of God the moment we most need it.
- We're not mindful of who we are in Christ, so we're easily beaten back into a cave of insecurity and inaction.
- We try to manage and cover the tracks of our sin, so our sin winds up managing us and smothering us with shame.
- We gather foolish friends around us, so every time we attempt to make changes, we get pulled down to their level.
- We stopped taking risks, so we've settled for a life guided by mediocrity and the expectations of others.
- We lack focus around our unique calling and gifting, so we find ourselves aiming at nothing and hitting it.
- We don't redeem time, so we see our days swallowed up by others' expectations and squandered by our weaknesses.

Many of us are suffering from a cracked cistern; our lives are leaking. Spiritual impotence has gone mainstream, and we know it. Claiming God's name but living like He's powerless to change us is too typical. The fulfillment of the promises of abundant life (John 10:10) and lives that produce "much fruit" (John 15:8) is something we desperately want. But rather than experiencing overflowing joy, we've settled for sips of happiness. Little addictions become welcome relief from our nagging failings. We've resigned ourselves to a bitter deception—it's sometimes better to settle for less and live in secret than run the risk of experiencing more shame. But here's the hope we can hold on to: when we've come to the end of ourselves, we're strategically positioned for God to show His power.

Chapter 2

RECOVERY

◊

We are products of our past, but we don't have to be prisoners of it.[1]

Rick Warren

Honest questions are a good thing. Here are a few: What makes one person's life hold water while the other person's leaks? How does someone take hold of God's promises and another find them to be frustratingly elusive? Why do some find breakthroughs and others stay in the sin-repent cycle? Finding the answers begins with realizing we're all in recovery.

I have a great love for "recovery ministry." It's generally composed of a wonderfully powerful group of people who have amazing stories of God's grace. They are committed to helping others heal from their hurts, habits, and hang-ups. And if you want to find a dynamic, authentic, and trusted friend, a recovery ministry is a great pool to go fishin' in.

But I don't like the name "recovery ministry"! What I struggle with is the spiritual caste system it inadvertently creates. We categorize issues like alcoholism, drug abuse, anger, divorce, sex addiction, and a few others as bad enough to warrant "recovery." That hurts us all because it separates "us" from "those recovery folks."

This is dangerous for three reasons:

1. We signal that some sins are worse than others and leave many other debilitating sins unaddressed. In the darkness, sins like gossip, envy, and pride only grow.

2. We lose the joy of embracing our common depravity—that we have all sinned and fall short. What's lost is that everyone is overcoming and everyone can be celebrating.

3. We send a message that if you commit certain sins, you need deep honesty and a close community. But if not, you can make it on your own.

Let me pull the curtains back so we can take a look at life as it really is for you and me. We all have sinned. We are all broken people. No one has arrived.

WE'RE ALL IN RECOVERY!

Everybody needs help and healing, not just those in recovery ministry. This is good news for serial gossipers, reckless leaders, recovering perfectionists, drive-by accusers, professional victims, and self-elevating embellishers. I have battled with most of these over my lifetime.

The broken pieces of your life are not lost on God. And God never condemns us; He patiently re-forms us. God sees two things at all times: 1. The new heart and nature He placed within His kids. He sees the righteousness of Christ in our lives that we received by believing Jesus and surrendering to Him. 2. He also sees the road we are walking and that we haven't arrived. The broken pieces we have from living in a broken world are real.

God and His children have something in common: a deep passion for getting our lives aligned with our new nature. Whether your destructive patterns are inherited, adopted, or even invented, God sees. Every challenge you face—God sees. All the goals you've set and never reached—God sees. The secret sins you try to manage—God sees. And the substitute gods you snuggle up to in hopes of dulling the pain—God sees it all. But wait for it—He knows, He cares, He loves, and He has a path forward!

Behavior patterns can chain us to a life cycle of sin-repent—but the cycle can be broken. Over my last thirty-five years of spiritual leadership, I've seen that events or weekend services can be a massive catalyst for change, but there must be systemic internal shifts. For us to become all we can be, we need the "D" word.

DISCIPLESHIP WAS INTENDED TO BE TRANSFORMATIONAL, BUT WE'VE MADE IT INFORMATIONAL.

RECLAIMING DISCIPLESHIP

Oh no! This heading, reclaiming discipleship, might cause you to set this book down. I don't like it either—it sounds outdated, academic, and boring. I envision a course with a curriculum held on a Saturday morning. There's cheap coffee and glazed donuts, and attendance is dwindling as the weeks go by. You and I keep coming because we don't want the instructor to feel bad.

I believe I actually know why discipleship gets such a bad rap. Discipleship was intended to be transformational, but we've made it informational. We've reduced discipleship to a class to take, a book to read, or a small group to join. All of those are great, but they come up short of God's goal.

God has a plan for breaking destructive, flawed, and failed systems. True discipleship isn't without pain. Even grape-producing branches in a vineyard are pruned to produce far more grapes. And Jesus promises to prune our life, "that it may bear more fruit" (John 15:2). Pain is a necessary element for your life to count for something great. Discipleship is God's plan for abundance; anything less is spectatorship. Dietrich Bonhoeffer said it even more directly: "Christianity without discipleship is always Christianity without Christ."[2]

Being a disciple of Jesus is more than an event; it's a lifestyle that invites God to touch and cut away at every aspect of who we are. Discipleship involves the intentionality of the Christian to bring broken systems before God and let Him prune, lift, and redirect our lives. If you desire God's promises in part or total, you must be a disciple. It is not optional. *Disciple* or *follower* are the words most used in the New Testament to describe what it is to have a relationship with God. Check out this little graph, and let it sink in.

How many times are these words used in the New Testament?
Christian = 3
Believer = 8
Disciple/follower = 269

Discipleship is the best descriptor of authentic faith. It indicates movement and engagement. It means that when we put our feet on the floor in the morning, we're allowing God to take control of our body and soul. It isn't "high road" faith; it's common faith. I'm begging you to decide to take hold of this kind of faith. Speak it out to God right now. Lean into discipleship, resolving to stay postured in His presence and walking in His power!

Before we get into how this all comes together, I want to encourage you. I want you to catch a vision of how resolve and simple spiritual training can change your life dramatically.

Greek poet Archilochus put life change in terms we can quickly grasp: "We don't rise to the level of our expectations; we fall to the level of our training."[3] It's true! Set all the lofty goals you want, but if your habits and routines are shaky and your systems are broken, you'll never reach escape velocity, and you'll always fall back to earth. But resolve to train yourself in God's power, bit by bit, day by day, and you'll be amazed. Here are some shots of hope:

Build Small Habits for the Long Haul

You can want to run a marathon competitively, but until you put a plan in place to eat a healthy diet, start running, increase mileage weekly, and have consistency over several months, the marathon will happen without you. But build minisystems of scheduled run times and small habits (reps that become part of your DNA) of eating healthy, going to bed early, stretching daily, and you'll be amazed at the progress you make in a year. My bride, Junanne, is not a natural runner. As a matter of fact, she was a non-runner. But she completed two marathons with small healthy habits. Imagine spending just twelve minutes every day reading the Scriptures. In one year, you will have read the entire Bible, learning things about God that will give you wisdom and strength for the long haul.

Renew Your Mind

You can desire to overcome disabling negative thinking, but without the habit of renewing your mind with truth, you'll be stuck indefinitely. However, when you take the time to memorize a few key verses of what God says about you, rinse your mind with these truths, recite these truths aloud daily, and repeat this for as many months as necessary, you'll be cleansed of these negative thoughts. And you'll find your whole life conforming to these truths as well—not only deepening your understanding of who you are but also seeing dramatic shifts in the way you relate to God and others.

Chart a Course

You can receive a God-sized vision for your life that thrills you and breathes hope into your soul. But your God-sized vision will remain an unrealized dream until you break yourself away from the routine of time-devouring media; spend consistent time talking with God and maybe journaling what He shows you; gain wisdom from people who have pursued a similar vision; develop a charted path with waypoints and markers to hit along the way; and get back on the horse you fell off. Flip the script with small, healthy adjustments of journaling insights, agreeing with God on practical course corrections, charting your progress, and—*boom*!—blue sky breaks through.

Dallas Willard, one of the greatest thinkers on spiritual formation, says discipleship is "the greatest opportunity individual human beings have in life and the only hope corporate mankind has of solving its insurmountable problems."[4] Here it is tightened down: *Discipleship is the greatest opportunity to solve insurmountable problems.* You want this! I believe the 7 Resolutions will help you experience it.

THE SECRET

There's one thing Satan and his demonic forces don't want us to discover—the secret to change that lasts a lifetime. Here's the single most important thing I've learned about true and sustained life change: **people who walk through life in the same way they were saved by Him—broken, humble, and entirely dependent—always win!** Let me give you two promises:

1. Any attempt to apply these resolutions in your strength will fail.

2. If you embrace your weaknesses and join God, you will prevail.

I'm so grateful that God allowed me to discover the secret of greatness. The chief characteristic that will make or break the application of this book is humility. Andrew Murray rocked me with this quote from his book *Humility*: "Humility is the only soil in which the graces root. Thus the lack of humility is the sufficient explanation of every defect and failure."[5] That's it!

Humility is not a sidebar. When we feel crushed by our sin, underwhelmed with ourselves, and overcome by God's grace, we are positioned for a radical revolution to begin.

So if you believe we're all in recovery and our only posture can be humility, you're in for a great ride.

The only challenge is that we're not naturally wired for humility. Everything we've learned in life has taught us that greatness is reached by climbing. When we think greatness, we think blue ribbon, top of the class, gold medal, six-pack abs, high compensation, and the list goes on.

These aren't inherently evil, and oftentimes they're the result of God's grace and a good work ethic. But our natural-born assessment of greatness leaves us striving, reaching, and climbing, even to the point of exhaustion.

God's plan for greatness is totally unique, and everyone can get a piece of the action. That's because it's not about climbing; it's about descending!

Here's God's plan for greatness: "Whoever humbles himself like this child is the greatest in the kingdom of heaven" (Matt. 18:4). It's this simple. In God's economy, self-actualization, self-determination, self-gratification, and most of the other "self-ations" have no place at the table of true greatness. This is for one simple reason: the people who experience God's promises have found that a Christ-dependence beats self-dependence every single day.

GOD'S PLAN FOR GREATNESS IS TOTALLY UNIQUE. . . . THAT'S BECAUSE IT'S NOT ABOUT CLIMBING; IT'S ABOUT DESCENDING!

We were made for something more than we can achieve in our own strength. We were designed to be conduits of transcendence. God never once knocks true greatness, he just defines it and shows us the way to achieve it. And when we become "like a child," we position ourselves for this greatness. That posture is utter dependence.

Sometimes God puts His truth on display in stunning ways. It was the first of three services on Sunday morning in Little Rock, Arkansas. I was back in town as a guest to preach a message on humility and dependence on God. The prep team asked me if I needed anything before I went on stage. It was short notice, but I asked if they could round me up a prop—one small child.

This church was on it. In five minutes, they brought me a ten-month-old little guy in the coolest OshKosh overalls. His mom was holding him, and I gave her the plan. After I read the verse on the greatness of childlike humility, I'd walk to the back of the stage to grab the little guy.

It couldn't have worked better. I carried him out to the center of that huge stage, crouched down, sat him on my knee, and concluded my challenge to become childlike. I said that although we are truly helpless in ourselves to take hold of all that God has, as we recognize our inabilities, become spiritual children, and reach out in dependence on God, amazing things will happen. When those last words came out of my lips, the little guy slowly reached straight up looking through the lights like he was reaching out to God. The whole auditorium gasped and then cheered. It was amazing!

Want true greatness? Don't settle another day for the best life you can make for yourself. God has more. Realize your need for someone bigger, stronger, and yes, greater than you. Become the child of God you are. Reach out to Him from a posture of need, and witness Him fill you up with all He has. God has a plan for true greatness, and you can have it.

C. S. Lewis got it right: "We are far too easily pleased."[6] It's time to get a grip on our lives and experience God's promises. Never settle for too little. If Christ has genuinely transformed you, there is something new in you. It's time to get your life aligned with God and come alive!

Chapter 3

THE 7 RESOLUTIONS

◊

Being sensible that I am unable to do anything without God's help, I do humbly entreat him by his grace to enable me to keep these Resolutions, so far as they are agreeable to his will, for Christ's sake.[1]

Jonathan Edwards

When I was a little guy, it was my job to get wood for the family fireplace. I usually tackled this in the light of day. One day, I forgot, and when evening came, the fire needed wood. Into the darkness I walked, and the night terrorized me. I got halfway to the woodpile and froze. Between our new family dog, snarling and lunging from the end of his chain, and the giant, reaching shadows of birch trees in the moonlight, I was paralyzed with fear. Somehow, I spun around and ran back to the house and up the stairs, where my father was reading the paper. He saw my panic. My good dad didn't need the details; he could see the terror in my eyes.

Without instilling an ounce of shame, Dad walked me outside and down the path to the woodpile. I stuck so close to him that I thought we were one. Confidence welled up inside. I had fresh eyes on the situation. What a victory to come striding back to the house with arms filled with firewood—looking over my shoulder at the defeated dog, knowing I'd won. And I was laughing inside at the giants that couldn't attack me.

AN ACT OF FAITH IS A GOOD THING, BUT A LIFE OF FAITH IS EVERYTHING.

The 7 Resolutions are agreements with God to walk with Him in lightness and darkness. Real faith acknowledges and embraces moments of fear and invites God to help us. Admitting weakness and leaning into the strength of God is what you were made for. Faith never outgrows the need for utter dependence. True faith is blown away by the power of God to both save us and transform us. Faith repents in the crisis of self-reliance and runs to God. Dependence is a way of living—because an act of faith is a good thing, but a life of faith is everything.

I want you to dream for a moment. Imagine getting honest enough to admit that you have life systems that are hurting you, and the ones you love are holding you back from your calling. Now imagine living out these 7 Resolutions and that the accompanying statements are true of you. Go ahead, get a vision for stepping into a future where your life is being changed.

THE 7 RESOLUTIONS

JOIN GOD

You are partnering with God and experiencing His power.

THINK TRUTH

Your mind is being renewed and freed from destructive thinking.

KILL SIN

You're finally putting to death those sins that have been killing you.

CHOOSE FRIENDS

You have quality people around you who help you live the abundant life.

TAKE RISKS

You now live in a way that puts your faith in motion and gives you energy.

FOCUS EFFORT

Your direction is clear because you're focused on your passion and gifting.

REDEEM TIME

You spend your time in a way that reflects your values and impacts the world.

BEFORE YOU BEGIN

I know something about adventures—travel, outdoor, mission. Think of me as your guide on a spiritual adventure. Before taking off on an adventure, guides always go over some ground rules and answer any questions of their fellow adventurers. Here are some questions you might have about the 7 Resolutions.

Should I See the 7 Resolutions as Sequential?

Yes and no. You'll notice a natural progression in the 7 Resolutions. One straightforward way to see this is that Take Risks, Focus Effort, and Redeem Time come after Join God, Think Truth, Kill Sin, and Choose Friends. This is because the active living out of our dreams has a better chance of truly being God-inspired and God-directed when we've taken hold of those first four resolutions.

Along with a natural progression, there will undoubtedly be specific resolutions you chose to focus on in different seasons. The 7 Resolutions Assessment is a highly predictive tool that will help pinpoint your resolutions of strength and weakness. (The 7 Resolutions Assessment is available for free at 7resolutions.com.)

Is There a Specific Way to Apply the 7 Resolutions?

Yes, there is an application section at the end of each chapter. I encourage you to read the whole book through, and then come back to work on the application points for each resolution. The nuance of actions taken will be distinct to each person's life situation. My confidence is that God will bring conviction from each resolution and specific direction for how you apply it to your life. For instance, whether you Join God through prayer walks with your spouse or friend, or you hit your knees in your bedroom with your Bible and prayer journal open, the ultimate goal is cultivating a conversation with God and hearing His voice.

Are the 7 Resolutions a Book . . . or Something More?

My prayer is that your experience goes beyond a book you read and becomes a lifestyle you choose—a personal revolution. We don't need more information; we need transformation. Because this book reflects how I personally Focus Effort in my life, I provide more resources and support for each resolution that can't be included in this book. You'll find more information on the resource page. My hope is that these resolutions become a part of who you are.

What Approach to the 7 Resolutions Will Help Bear the Most Fruit?

This is critical! Choose to be humble and stay there. Humility is all you should bring to the table; without it, nothing can be won. Humility is not a gift from God that we wait to fall in our lap. It's a choice to make, and it's the most crucial decision you can make every day. Remember Andrew Murray's words that sent me to my knees: "The lack of humility is the sufficient explanation of every defect and failure."[2]

Pride is not something God accepts. He'll resist pride because proud people can only move in their strength. But humble people are given God's favor (1 Peter 5:5). If you desire God to overthrow the broken systems in your life, you have a move to make. Humble yourself under God's strong and loving hand, and He will ultimately lift you and take you places you could never have gone before (1 Peter 5:6).

The pressure is off. Rules to follow, behavior modification, sheer grit, and self-will can never bring lasting change. God transforms our lives the same way God saves our lives—through total and complete dependence on Him. Working in our own strength just proves we've taken the bait of Satan (Gal. 3:1).

This isn't to say you have nothing to do. But all you do must be in the wake of what God has done and in His power alone. It's time to let God show His love toward you and display His power in you.

Chapter 4

RESOLUTION #1
JOIN GOD

◊

If God be your partner, make your plans large![1]

D. L. Moody

It's a simple concept. There is a boat with a strong motor. Clipped to the stern of the boat is a rope that is seventy feet in length. At the end of the rope is a handle. The person in the water with skis on has one job: Hold on to the handle. Yell "hit it." Let the boat pull you to the surface so you can do what is called water skiing.

It looked easy enough.

The water was cold, but I was amped up and ready to go. Buoyed with a flotation vest and the tips of my skis pointing to the sky, I gripped the handle. As the rope pulled tight, I yelled, "Hit it!" The boat engine roared, and immediately I felt the resistance. Arms straight, I sensed myself coming up out of the lake. Then I did it. I broke the rule of waterskiing 101. I thought I'd help myself get to the surface a little more quickly, so I tried to pull myself up. In an instant, I was coming out of my skis and getting a full nasal flush—I had to let go.

The boat circled. My friends were chuckling a bit, but the adult on board gave me the best and most straightforward advice. "Karl, just lean back, extend your arms, hold on, and don't try to pull yourself up; let the boat do the work." The rope became taut, and again, I yelled, "Hit it!" This time I kept my arms straight and let the boat do what only the boat could do—pull me up out of that lake and take me on a most incredible trip—I was water skiing!

We make the same mistake in our relationship with God. Somehow we believe we can get ourselves up and go in our strength. But worse, we think it's our job to get up or help God in some way—the urge to use our power is strong. This tendency to take God's role in our lives and try to assist in some way is very natural. In a broken world, we've been trained to believe that if anything is going to get fixed or a situation changed, we have to do it.

Some people don't want to have a thing to do with God—they don't believe He exists. Other people try to do something for God—they hope to gain His approval. But another group, possibly small, has discovered that God invites us to partner with Him. They know that the pressure is off. This group has nothing to prove. Gone are the days of trying to make God happy with us. This group has learned that we are friends of Jesus and the real power for living comes by joining God.

But we're called to live supernaturally. Merriam-Webster defines *supernatural* as "of or relating to an order of existence beyond the visible observable universe."[2] Joining God is reaching "beyond the visible" and taking hold of power you don't possess. In resolving to join God, you're saying yes to living in a new manner that liberates you from striving and trying harder to live the life of a disciple of Christ. "For it is God who works in you, both to will and to work for his good pleasure" (Phil. 2:13). Let this little verse come fully alive in your mind, and it will be one of the greatest epiphanies you've ever experienced—it was for me. God wants to reorder your life in a way that trusts, rests, and relies on His strength. God is inviting you to partner with God and experience His power. Let God's Spirit do the work!

TWICE SAVED

God saved me twice. The first time He saved my soul. The second time He broke me free from the prison of performance—thinking I had something to prove, gain, or lose. I was trying to pull myself up. My soul was secure; it was striving in my strength to live the Christian life that was giving me fits. If Satan can't keep us from going to heaven when we die, he certainly wants to keep us from living in God's power until we die.

This spiritual battle for trying to live the Christian life in our strength is best seen in Galatians 3:1–3:

> O foolish Galatians! Who has bewitched you? It was before your eyes that Jesus Christ was publicly portrayed as crucified. Let me ask you only this: Did you receive the Spirit by works of the law or by hearing with faith? Are you so foolish? Having begun by the Spirit, are you now being perfected by the flesh?

They so lacked wisdom that Paul called them foolish. It was a "bewitching" deception that originated from Satan. The deception was that they needed to live by the law all over again. Paul asked them if God's power was enough to save them but not enough to sanctify (grow) them. Then he appealed to them to live life in the same power that saved their life—the Spirit of God!

You face the same spiritual battle, and it's probably daily—the struggle to allow the God who *saved you* to continue to *change you*. We are only saved by the Spirit's power, and yet we try to get sanctified in our power. It's downright foolish! Growing up and attempting to produce spiritual fruit in our strength will never succeed, and it's exhausting.

I was working hard at a spiritual life full of achievement but fell far short of abundance. God saw all my trying, striving, hoop-jumping, and box-checking and stepped into the noise and busyness of life to save me from me again. He spoke to a hollow place in my heart and offered to lift the weight to give me rest. He saved me, this time from my efforts to produce fruit in my life—that was His job!

God had to overhaul my thinking on how I lived my spiritual life. Somewhere along my journey, I had adopted a destructive perspective on growth. The words "I should," "I ought to," "keep trying, Karl," and other heavy-yoked terms weighed on my mind and were muttered from my lips. I saw Bible reading, prayer, study, fasting, and all the other spiritual disciplines as things I should do to please God. This was a destructive way of thinking. God was already pleased with me. But I was busy trying to earn approval from God and others, and it left me empty.

The best way for me to illustrate this is to take you onto a commercial fishing boat. For eight seasons, I commercially fished off the coast of Alaska. Things can get dicey and dangerous quickly on these coastal waters. Our VHF (very high frequency) radio was a lifeline. To communicate with other boats, and especially the ship we delivered our fish to, we needed a VHF radio.

One late evening our boat became swallowed in a fog. With a boatload of salmon, we needed to get back to the ship and off-load. My captain radioed the ship: Where are you? Can we come by to off-load? On which side of the ship do you want us to off-load—port or starboard?

My captain pressed the button on the handheld microphone to speak, lifted the button, waited for a response, then pressed the button and confirmed that he understood. Three times he did this simple exercise. Soon we were at the ship on the port side, the salmon got off-loaded, and the ship captain invited us up for a cup of coffee in the galley.

My disconnect with God was that I wasn't letting go of the button like my captain did when he wanted to hear from the ship's deck. I was just holding it down and going as hard as I could. I thought I was doing well. I was busy praying to God but not letting Him respond. I was reading His Word but not listening for His voice. I was even fasting for short spurts but not taking the time to hear His words of wisdom. I was busy doing ministry, quite effective ministry, but not with Him. God was inviting me to join Him in life, love, *and* ministry.

With the help of a friend, a few key passages of Scripture, some rich saints who had authored deep-water books many years ago, and the power of the Holy Spirit, I felt like God was saving me again—this time from striving and trying to live the Christian life in my efforts.

A fresh understanding of God's truth was sending me soaring. The God-inspired words of Galatians 2:20 now lifted me up me like never before: "It is no longer I who live, but Christ who lives in me." This meant that living my life and taking hold of God's promises was not on me. The mad scramble to perform was over. The rabid need for my vision to get implemented in my strength or managing how I would be perceived was evaporating. I could rest in the confidence that God had my back, Jesus had my heart, and the Holy Spirit was filling me with power.

All my study, conversations, and wrestling had finally converged. The scales were falling from my eyes, and I could hardly believe it. The liberty was terrific.

To get off this treadmill of self-help spirituality, God had to slow me down. Taking time for prayer walks with Junanne was a big breakthrough. Speaking with the two people I loved the most and listening to her and God was so refreshing. Bible study took a turn. I now have a habit of genuinely listening to the Spirit of God as I study and read. I've told my bride for years now that the Word pops off the page and into my heart as I humbly wait for the Spirit's voice. God has me seeing the truth and understanding it like I couldn't in my strength.

Joining God rather than busting your tail for God is both refreshing and fruitful. I make better decisions. I'm able to apply the Word more accurately. And when I talk with God, I know His voice, and I follow Him. What's best is I now understand and live out 1 Thessalonians 5:17, "pray without ceasing." I'm never in a meeting alone with one other person. God is always with me. I find God nudging me to confront something or not. To speak or be silent. To extend words of love or just listen. It's a real-time relationship with the God of the universe.

Am I always aware of His presence in prayer, reading, meeting, singing, or leading? No. I head out on my own often. I still pray, study, and go through life without letting go of the button to listen. But God calls me back to that place of freedom and power. I love getting a callout from God to get up and go on a mini-date with my wife. Yes, God's Spirit has prompted me to leave what I'm doing and make a call, send a text, or any number of things, including a quick mini-date with Junanne. When I respond to God, I'm always satisfied beyond words. And yes, when I get out on a surprise date, my bride feels loved, and I feel refreshed. There's nothing like joining God.

SPIRITUAL DISCIPLINES ARE NOT HOW WE PROVE OUR LOVE FOR GOD; THEY'RE WHERE GOD PROVES HIS LOVE FOR US.

Learning my need to join God was frightening and freeing. I now believe that spiritual disciplines are either powerful or powerless—there is no middle ground. How we *approach* prayer, study, fasting, meditation, and any other discipline will dictate their value. If we approach them like we're joining God going in, we will become a different person coming out. This is how God reframed my thinking on spiritual growth, and I share it now frequently: spiritual disciplines are not how we prove our love for God; they're where God proves His love for us.

Here are the three things God wanted me to see. These core truths began to help me shift my mindset away from working for God in my strength. As I agree with God, I'm starting to join God and trust in His power. Each of these will be unpacked in the pages ahead.

1. Humility is a vital baseline for everything we do.
2. Proximity to Jesus is our only hope of producing fruit.
3. Saving grace gives us new life; training grace gives us abundant life.

I was being released from my striving. I knew that I didn't need to bring something to the table to gain approval or even be productive. Exchanging the heavy yoke for the light yoke that Jesus spoke of was finally making sense. To stop seeing Bible study, prayer, meditation, fasting, and other disciplines as means of proving myself to God or validating myself to others was a huge relief. God wanted me to join Him and stop pulling myself up by my spiritual bootstraps.

But I faced a make-or-break decision that would determine whether my life would produce "much" spiritual fruit. Would I stay postured for God's power or return to living in my strength? This is not an over-spiritualization of your life: Satan wants to drag as many people with him into a dark eternity as possible. And those he can't drag away, he tempts to live independent of God—ineffective and unfruitful.

POSITIONED FOR POWER

The instincts and nature we're born with run in the opposite direction of spiritual growth and victory. Self-promotion, self-protection, self-aggrandizement, and self-help are what come naturally to us. But God's way is 180 degrees opposite. Jesus said, "The greatest among you shall be your servant" (Matt. 23:11). Everything in God's economy is upside down and backward. But when we choose to live in submission to God's economy, we benefit exponentially.

The beauty of humility is that it's not actually a demotion, it's a promotion. Jesus said it clearly: "Whoever exalts himself will be humbled, and whoever humbles himself will be exalted" (Matt. 23:12). Many mistakenly think humility is to degrade ourselves. But that would fly in the face of our new identity. Humility is to come under God's authority, live in His economy, and let Him carry us to victory.

It's not about thinking pitifully little of ourselves; it's about thinking of ourselves less because we're captivated by God's glory and our joy in Him. It's the nature of Christ to not be served but to serve. This is why humility is possibly the most important decision of those who are rich in faith.

God has given us free will—the power to decide. Humility is essential to living near to God. If you want to have a partnership with God, to live in His grace and power, humility is the choice that makes it happen. Joining God doesn't happen without it. Just look at these vivid examples.

- "God opposes the proud but gives grace to the humble." (James 4:6)
- "For though the LORD is high, he regards the lowly, but the haughty he knows from afar." (Ps. 138:6)
- "Humble yourselves, therefore, under the mighty hand of God so that at the proper time he may exalt you." (1 Peter 5:6)

It's clear from Scripture, and we've all felt it. Humility closes the gap between us and God that pride had created. And when that gap is closed, we experience promotion and exaltation. I've had men ask me why they feel like their prayers go nowhere. Sometimes it's because they go nowhere. God loves His kids enough to be silent in the face of our pride. All of our natural striving takes us further down, but choose humility, and you'll join God!

One day I witnessed a guy nearly drown to death in what would have been the most horrific way. It was summer in Anchorage, Alaska.

Dad took me fishing downtown at Ship Creek. There were a few fishermen and plenty of salmon to go around. The one thing that can kill you at Ship Creek is the tides. The tides can rise well over twenty feet from low to high, twice a day. You visibly see the waters rise, and they move like a swift river. If you're not alert, the tides sweep you away to your death.

We had just arrived, and the tide was turning. Dad noticed a man struggling to walk up the bank through the mud and silt. Then it got serious. With every effort to lift a leg free, the opposite leg sank more deeply into the mud. He was stuck. My dad knew we had to move fast. He threw a rope to the now distressed man and told him to tie it around his waist. Dad tied the other end around the bumper of our old Rambler. He yelled one instruction to the poor guy, "Lay down in the mud, and let me pull you out gently!" The man stopped struggling in his strength, lay down, and took hold of the rope, leaving his rod and tackle box behind. We pulled him to high ground. Within minutes, the place where he had been standing was covered in water. Lying down and taking hold of the rope allowed him to avoid the fate of many who have seen the tidewaters of Alaska slowly take their life.

The spiritual parallels here are easy to see:

- All self-effort that ignores the need for God will ultimately be swamped by the incoming tide of time. We don't have much time, and there is no time for pride.

- People who resist God's help put themselves in peril. Some have been injured, and others have perished. All who resist joining God will one day wish they'd humbled themselves.

- Those who are willing to lay down your life as "a living sacrifice" (Rom. 12:1) will discover the hand of God lifting them from the deepest pain and challenges they face.

I've learned a valuable lesson in the last few years that impacts every area of my life with blessings I could never have imagined. The way you come to Jesus is the way you grow in Jesus—on your knees in total humility. Look how humility is championed in Scripture:

- "God opposes the proud but gives grace to the humble." (1 Peter 5:5)
- "When pride comes, then comes disgrace, but with the humble is wisdom." (Prov. 11:2)
- "The fear of the LORD is instruction in wisdom, and humility comes before honor." (Prov. 15:33)
- "Before destruction a man's heart is haughty, but humility comes before honor." (Prov. 18:12)
- "Humble yourselves before the Lord, and he will exalt you." (James 4:10)
- "He has told you, O man, what is good; and what does the LORD require of you but to do justice, and to love kindness, and to walk humbly with your God?" (Mic. 6:8)
- "The reward for humility and fear of the LORD is riches and honor and life." (Prov. 22:4)

You may think that humility is going to rip you off. That to choose to be humble is to settle for too little. Nothing could be further from the truth. But sometimes, we benefit from hearing testimony from someone who has street credibility. Saint Augustine speaks from profound experience: "Do you wish to rise? Begin by descending. You plan a tower that will pierce the clouds? Lay first the foundation of humility."[3]

You would be wise to take time at this moment to agree with God and to choose humility. Watch what God will drag you up out of and the rock He wants to set you on. Witness where He'll put your feet. Feel the relief that will flood your soul for what you have avoided and what lies ahead.

THE GAME CHANGER

Weakness and our inability are a commodity in God's economy. One passage has made me a champion of weakness more than any other. In 2 Corinthians 12, Paul struggled with something that was causing him pain, distraction, or both. The answer Paul got was the answer I needed back then, and it fuels me to this day. God's power was perfected, not in my denying or covering up weakness, but by embracing weakness. *Boom*! That's it, the critical element in God's plan for abundance is weakness. This flipped my world upside down.

Jesus told the most epic metaphor of joining God. It's cited in John 15. I use this when speaking or broadcasting as often as possible. Jesus is giving the last instructions to His first disciples. The metaphor is an absolute game changer for every disciple of Christ since. To me, it's so vivid that if you hear it or see it accurately, you'll live it the rest of your life. This is what Jesus said:

> Abide in me, and I in you. As the branch cannot bear fruit by itself, unless it abides in the vine, neither can you, unless you abide in me. I am the vine; you are the branches. Whoever

> abides in me and I in him, he it is that bears much fruit, for **apart from me you can do nothing**. . . . By this my Father is glorified, that you bear much fruit and so prove to be my disciples." (John 15:4–5, 8)

I often grab two volunteers and bring them on stage to illustrate this teaching of Jesus. I put one person in the role of Jesus. They are to stand there and be the gnarly vine that comes up out of the ground and has all the life-giving supply a branch will need. Then I ask the other person to be the branch. This is simple. They put one hand on the vine, touching "Jesus." With the other hand, they extend in the air in the opposite direction. Now the Scriptures can make perfect sense. The branch (you and me whom God has saved) has two choices on where to focus: 1. We can focus on the performance/production where the grapes are to grow (our extended hand away from Jesus); 2. Or we can focus on proximity to Jesus—abiding in close relationship with Him (our hand that is touching Jesus). Pick #1 or #2, but you can't do both.

This is your big decision; it's the game changer. Either you abide and have proximity to Jesus or try to perform and produce fruit in your strength. Every time we try to grow fruit and rely on our energy, we come up empty and resign ourselves to paste fake fruit onto our lives. There's a bigger problem with counterfeit fruit and pretending we're producing fruit. Those at a distance may think we look pretty good, but those closest to us see our lives for what they are. No one is compelled to follow Jesus if all they see is fake fruit.

Living in our strength, we find ourselves struggling to do things that are only born of God. Being friendly and biting your tongue is a far cry from having peace and self-control—the former is the fruit of the flesh and the latter the fruit of the Spirit. If we focus our attention on trying to produce much fruit, we will utterly fail because Jesus said "apart from me you can do nothing."

The real hope we have for a fruitful life is to agree to join God. By continuously clinging to God, we will look over one day to see our lives bearing fruit that blows our minds. You are a branch if Christ has saved you. Now the only question is: What end of the branch will you focus on? Performance is exhausting and unfruitful. Proximity pays enormous dividends—join God.

GRACE OR BUST

I've made over a hundred round trips from Anchorage, Alaska, to the "Lower Forty-Eight," as it's called in Alaska. Eight of those trips were *driving* along the hair-raising Alaska-Canadian Highway (ALCAN).

In the late sixties, my parents would take the economy approach to travel and load the whole family into a car, even if it meant thousands of miles of driving; flying was too much on my dad's teacher's salary. But heading south on the ALCAN was no small feat. Rough gravel, dangerous cliffs, no shoulders, rockslides, and sinkholes were standard. Broken windshields, flat tires, running out of gas, and sometimes sinking into mud ruts were expectations of every traveler.

There was one thing that made all the difference for some travelers. *The MILEPOST*. This thick book gave us every bit of information for refueling, repairs, survival, landmarks, motels, food stops, times to travel, and even sights to see. If you had *The MILEPOST*, you had everything you needed to get where you were going.

Grace is to the Christian traveler what *The MILEPOST* was to the ALCAN traveler. Grace not only saves us, but it also carries us. I've often heard grace called "unmerited favor." I like it, but it's not as robust as grace truly is. Grace is God's power at work in us, to do through us what we could never see or do in our strength. Grace is not a theory or buzzword. It is the actual power of God ready to be unleashed in the life of any person who sees their inability and surrenders to God's capability. For years, I had believed there was saving grace, but I'd never really known or lived in God's grace and power for growth. I actually lived like "God saves; I work to grow." Oh, how I missed it!

As the fullness of God's grace began to unfold, two verses illuminated grace in a whole new way. Because of these two verses, I began to see grace everywhere in the Scriptures, and not just for saving lives, but also for growing lives that experienced God in power. Here are the verses:

> For the **grace** of God has appeared, bringing **salvation** for all people, **training** us to renounce ungodliness and worldly passions, and to live self-controlled, upright, and godly lives in the present age. (Titus 2:11–12)

Look at this! There is one grace of God. It's for saving and training—grace brings us from death to life, and grace trains us to grow strong in this life and gets us to our eternal home in power. This was revolutionary for me. It overthrew my flawed thinking about how life works for God's kids. I knew well the power of God's saving grace, but I had never fully grasped that His grace wanted to train us "to live self-controlled, upright, and godly lives in the present age."

Everything made more sense now; training grace started showing up in nearly every story and narrative in Scripture. Training grace is a neglected gift of God. Especially in cultures where self-sufficiency is celebrated more than interdependency.

No place is our need for training grace more evident than Paul's letter to the church of Galatia. Paul hated striving in the flesh (our strength) as much as we do. Living to please God in our power is futile, and Paul is passionate about crushing this self-deception. Paul's letter to the Galatians reveals two common problems with grace that we face and what the solution is for each.

***Problem:* We can be reborn by grace and walk away from grace.** "I am astonished that you are so quickly deserting him who called you in the grace of Christ and are turning to a different gospel." (Gal. 1:6)
***Solution:* We can only live this life by trusting Christ's work in us.** "I have been crucified with Christ. It is no longer I who live, but Christ who lives in me. And the life I now live in the flesh I live by faith in the Son of God, who loved me and gave himself for me." (Gal. 2:20)

***Problem:* We can be fooled into trying to live in our strength.** "Are you so foolish? Having begun by the Spirit, are you now being perfected by the flesh?" (Gal. 3:3)
***Solution:* We never need to return to the slavery of striving in our strength.** "But now that you have come to know God, or rather to be known by God, how can you turn back again to the weak and worthless elementary principles of the world, whose slaves you want to be once more?" (Gal. 4:9)

You might be thinking, "Karl, aren't we called to press on, run to win the prize, make every effort to add to our faith, and live by other Scriptures that speak of our effort?" And the answer is yes, but never apart from the grace and power of God. I love how Dallas Willard captured grace as a means of training: "Grace is not opposed to effort, it is opposed to earning."[4] Grace is how we join God in watching

Him genuinely change our lives. Agreeing to join God is practical and transformational. This is how it works.

GET THE SWING OF IT

I love golf, but I'll never be a great golfer; I'm okay with that. There came a time when I realized that for me to shoot consistently low scores, I'd have to increase my playing time tenfold. But the bigger problem was that the majority of that time would be spent practicing a new swing to correct the one that was flawed. Bad habits had been acquired, and I'd repeated them for so long they'd become a part of how I swung the club. Changing my swing would require some real intentionality. If I can play a couple of times a year, hit a few long drives, and sink a tricky putt, I'm happy. You have to make value calls in life.

Agreeing to join God is a big value call that's worth the investment. Joining God is the most challenging resolution for me to learn or relearn. It's like practicing a new golf swing but a whole lot more critical. Much of what we've learned or witnessed in our spiritual life was all about working in our strength. Striving is a common language spoken in church lobbies and small groups and even preached as the way to live. But relearning how to grow and journey with God is not optional—too much is on the line.

Over time I've noticed how all that's evil aims its arsenal at our mindset toward the spiritual disciplines. I often need to rehearse everything I've given you in this resolution because the battle to perform and live in my strength rages in my life, and you'll face this battle as well. It's common. Your "Join God" swing is tough but so worth it.

APPLICATION:
How to Join God

EMBRACE HUMILITY – This will position you to be strengthened with God's power as never before. True humility will lead you to serve, seek forgiveness, and respond more quickly to the voice of God. Choosing humility will unleash blessings.

- Ask God to search for pride in every area of your life.
- Journal what God's Spirit is convicting you of and be specific.
- If your pride has damaged any relationships, ask those folks for forgiveness.
- Tell God your desire to reach out, and join Him in shaping your life humbly.
- Repeat as needed!

BE THE BRANCH – The abiding life is the only life to live. Learning to live in proximity to Jesus and not performing for Him will revolutionize your life.

- Ask the Holy Spirit to reveal any striving activities you've grown accustomed to.
- Confess all past striving in your strength to God and agree how painful it's been.
- Tell Jesus that your heart's desire is to stay close to Him and not shut Him out.
- Share this new resolve with trusted friends or family who may have seen you attempting to fake the spiritual life in your strength.

- Tell God you are eager to watch Him bring "much fruit" from your life.

TAP INTO TRAINING GRACE — What a great discovery. The fact that God has both the power to *save us* and *train us* is a revolutionary discovery of how God works. Welcome to living daily by grace.

- Tell Satan that you're done taking his bait of striving, proving, and all attempts to pull yourself up in your strength.
- Boast to God that you are too weak to do what needs to be done in your life.
- Call to mind your most challenging/persistent area of weakness. Thank God that He is able to perfect His power in that exact area.
- Thank God that His grace holds the power to do in you what you could never do in yourself.

Chapter 5

RESOLUTION #2
THINK TRUTH

◊

We truly live at the mercy of our ideas.[1]
Dallas Willard

God was stirring and the word was spreading and people were seeking—some were just curious; others were in deep pain. At the top of the hour, the church's worship band opened with a big anthem of praise, and the spirit in the room was one of expectation. God had been showing up in power for weeks, and this night would be no different.

Then it happened. She walked into the auditorium filling up with worshipers. She turned the head of nearly every guy in the room. It's not like she was the only new girl that night or that she wanted the attention. We soon found out that was the last thing she wanted. But she was striking, and that was part of her story.

Jasmine was a true seeker. She had recently told God, "Show me you exist and that you love me, or I'm checking out of life." One beautiful breezy night, as Jasmine sat on the porch of her apartment, she was overwhelmed by pain and shame. "Give me a sign, God," she said. At that moment, God moved. He split the clouds, and there was the moon: full, clear, and almost sitting in Jasmine's lap. Jasmine loved the moon. It was like God looking into her eyes, saying, "I'm not done with you, so don't quit on yourself." That was all the sign Jasmine needed.

The following day she followed through on what she thought God told her. Jasmine reached out to find a place with people who might know the God who would drop the moon in her lap. That's how she discovered our large group of Jesus followers. We were young, passionate, authentic, and free. That was attractive to Jasmine, and although damaged by takers and users, she still found us to be believable.

I gave the message that night. As I wrapped up, we went into an extended time of worship. There were tears, laughter, and spontaneous applause. Stories of life change were shared between songs. And after every story, there was a roar that sounded more like it came from the crowd whose college basketball team had just hit a buzzer-beater for the win.

Jasmine wanted more.

Over the next few weeks, she watched, while behind the scenes God was at work in her heart. The night Jasmine surrendered to Jesus was memorable. As she whispered those words of repentance and belief, she held nothing back. Through sobs of joy and relief, Jasmine was changed.

My wife asked Jasmine if she wanted to learn who she was in Christ and how this new way of thinking would impact her day-to-day living. Jasmine was all in. Junanne suspected early on that Satan was playing mind games with her. But this was no game; Satan wasn't playing with Jasmine, he was trying to crush her. Jasmine was being bombarded with condemning thoughts. Her past hadn't caught up with her; it was always in front of her. The images and thoughts of the past haunted her mind and soul.

Her story was like too many others. Abused in her youth by her father, Jasmine learned early on that her body got her attention. The boys liked sex, but none of those relationships produced the intimacy and love she desired. Out of love and low on money, Jasmine decided she might as well sell what she was giving away. The partners multiplied, and the pain increased.

Jasmine needed to break free from the condemnation of her past sexual encounters.

Junanne set up a time to meet with Jasmine to help her win the battle for her mind. Junanne invited her own mentor to join them. Together, they helped Jasmine identify self-loathing thoughts and renounced them in Jesus' name.

When the three women went to their knees in prayer, they stayed there for many hours. Jasmine walked through the renunciation of every event and every name she could remember. The list was long. The tears were many, and the pain of facing the truth was deep but thorough. Junanne began to introduce Jasmine to who she was in Christ—her true new identity. Jasmine stood up from the floor a new woman. She understood how complete her salvation was and how God saw her. The darkest parts of her past were painted over with Christ's blood.

RESOLVING TO THINK THE TRUTH IS THE SINGLE MOST IMPORTANT RESOLUTION OF THE SEVEN.

Jasmine is unrecognizable from those days. She radiates freedom and joy. She married a great man and has a beautiful family. They live overseas now. Jasmine and her husband share a common passion with Junanne and me: making disciples and helping people get their minds around who they are in Christ.

Resolving to think the truth is the single most important resolution of the seven. Knowing who you are in Christ as a result of the new birth miracle and how to sort lies from truth is vital for discovering all that's new and what God has for you. If this resolution, Think Truth, had a spiritual equation, it would be this: when God does the work of saving, and we do the right thinking, we're on the path to abundant living.

TWO KINDS OF WRONG THINKING

For all the adventures I've experienced, I'm still afraid of heights. Something about even the remotest possibility of falling to my death freaks me out. This fear was on full display in high school when I joined a leisurely climb with friends that turned into something more. I got talked into ascending a mountain to explore an abandoned mine. To ascend the final one hundred meters and finally enter the cave opening, we had to walk up a high ridge. Fall to the right, and you die. Fall to the left, and you're better off falling to the right.

My buddies scampered up the narrow ridge like mountain goats. My turn! I dropped to my belly and hugged the ridge like a wet rag draped over a railing. I scooted slowly up, looking like a wimp but glad to be alive—my friends mocking me the whole way. Here's the point: Scooting up and hugging that ridge is a picture of clinging to our identity in Christ. To think the truth is to be aware of who you are in Christ and how you're moving through life. Cling to your identity in Christ because believing the lies of the world will hurt you or kill you. It's that simple.

Thinking truth and knowing who we are in Christ is so vital that we shouldn't even attempt to move on to the other resolutions until we've allowed God to stay our minds on this one. There are two ways we fall off the high ridge of standing in our true identity—two kinds of wrong thinking!

1. Self-loathing: Thinking less of ourselves than God thinks of us.

You can't look confidently at God because of your shame.

You think God is disgusted with you, and you understand.

You don't know how you could be used in the lives of others.

You look at God's promises and tell yourself, "Those aren't for me."

2. Self-elevating: Thinking more of ourselves than we think of God.

You look in the mirror and see your highest authority.

You think God is a great help to the life you're building.

You are focused on others primarily as a means to move up yourself.

You read the above three and self-implicate by saying, "This is never me."

God loves to put His power on display by cultivating humble thoughts where pride once ruled and conquering thoughts where defeat once ruled. He does this to show us that He's strong enough to bring down the prideful and gentle enough to lift the defeated.

EVEN JESUS HAD TO THINK TRUTH

Your mind is never out of control. It's either under the control of God and guided by the Holy Spirit (John 16:13) or under the influence of darkness and all that is evil. One of the most fundamental ways Satan aims to control us is through our minds. There's no real secret here. The battle is for the most dominant voice to be God's, knowing all demonic forces will try to counter the truth that sets us free.

Mind games are Satan's forte. He is so skilled at influencing our thoughts and directing our life away from God's best that he even tried to take out Jesus with his craft. This epic battle for control is described vividly by three New Testament authors and disciples of Christ, Matthew, Mark, and Luke, so it must be important!

Satan tried to twist the truth in three distinct ways. He tried to take down our Savior by suggesting shortcuts, appealing to celebrity, and flexing some power. The details of the temptations in the wilderness are as crucial as the tools Jesus had in His arsenal to fight them.

The Three Temptations of Christ

1. Shortcuts—Jesus was hungry after fasting for forty days. When Satan said, "Command these stones to become loaves of bread" (Matt. 4:3), Jesus quoted truth back at Satan: "Man shall not live by bread alone, but by every word that comes from the mouth of God" (Matt. 4:4). Jesus rejected the temptation to take a shortcut and waited for God to nourish the stomach and soul. So practical for you and me.

2. Celebrity—Satan then took Jesus to see all the kingdoms of the world. The deal was simple. "Fall down and worship me," Satan said, and then promised Jesus "glory" (Matt. 4:8–9). Jesus didn't take the bait. He shot back with "worship the Lord your God and him only shall you serve." Celebrity, both small and large scale, is a temptation Satan throws around today.

3. Power—When power is dangled as a temptation, a lot of people bite. Satan took Jesus to the pinnacle of the temple and added the dare, "'throw yourself down'" (Matt. 4:6). He wanted Jesus to put His power on display and show off the kind of command He had of the angels who would sweep under Him and protect Him. Jesus simply replied, "You shall not put the Lord your God to the test" (Matt. 4:7).

Satan left and began to plot a final attack. But get this. Jesus survived the desert and these three temptations because of two things: 1. He walked into the wilderness powered and guided by the Holy Spirit (see Matt. 4:1). 2. He was well-versed in truth so that He could fend off Satan's twisted lies (see Matt. 4:1–10). Yes, Jesus had to think truth!

You will not escape the battle for control of your mind in this life. Added to the demonic component is the baggage you've collected along the way. Reckless words from a parent that still echo in your ears. The friend who stepped on you to take a step up. That teacher, coach, or authority figure who told you what you would never be. You have been shaped and directed, oftentimes negatively, by the words and actions of culture, celebrities, cliques, and even the church crowd. Now bring a person to mind who was close to you, but you would never want to emulate. Even they've had a hand in shaping the way you think and what your mind dwells on.

What we think about most impacts the decisions and direction of our life. Think lies, and you'll fall. Think truth, and you'll arrive at God's calling and promises for your life. How to fight off these natural inclinations, accusations, and temptations is what this resolution is all about. Your mind being renewed by truth and freed from destructive thinking will equip you to tear down the lies you've believed and the lies that are yet to come.

"SHUT UP AND LISTEN!"

God's more of a gentleman than my first football coach. But I must admit, if the coach hadn't yelled at us that first week, we'd never have gotten a win that season. There we were, little guys, running around doing what we thought seemed right but looking like disoriented "bobblehead" figures more than football players. In the middle of chaos and confusion, Coach Sargent (no joking, that was his name), yelled, "Shut up and listen!" We were shaken and awakened. Some of us were scared. Then he quietly laid out for us the basics of football.

Coach Sargent explained the sidelines, yard markers, rules, positions, and plays. He spoke with passion and compassion. We believed him. When someone got cocky, he'd sit them down. When someone got down, he'd pick them up. We knew our team name and who we were as individual players. We knew he loved us. We saw him sad for us in our losses and thrilled for us in the few wins.

The start of the season was brutal. But we learned from our mistakes and kept listening to the coach. We were imperfect but getting stronger as the games ticked by. By the end of the season, we were like a glitch-free, high-speed smartphone. Everything was in sync because we knew who we were, where each of us fit, and win or lose Coach Sargent loved us.

There's a bunch of us disoriented "bobblehead" Christians who need to listen up. We've been drafted onto Team God, but we have yet to understand the importance of hearing His voice above all others. Some of us have wandered far afield. Others have just shut Him out. But I'm convinced most of us haven't learned the art of thinking right. Listening to God has seemed unproductive or unattainably transcendent. But it's biblical and accessible, and across the pages of Scripture, we see God giving us a vision for hearing His voice and thinking rightly. Here's just a few striking truths that when understood and applied will result in significant personal wins:

- What you think about will either bless you or kill you. (Rom. 8:6)
- God's blessing is always linked to listening. (1 Kings 11:38)
- Sober thinking people avoid being deceived and destroyed. (1 Peter 1:13)
- When we stop to remember, we will see God's character. (Ps. 48:9)
- Discerning right thinking from wrong thinking helps us obey God. (2 Cor. 10:5)
- Thinking rightly is the most critical factor in life transformation. (Rom. 12:1–2)
- What your mind thinks about will impact the trajectory of your life. (Phil. 4:9)

God is calling. He wants your attention. When your thinking is aligned with God, your mind is aimed at God's promises—every aspect of your life will be impacted powerfully. Knowing the enemies of thinking truth is a good thing. Bringing into the light what's beating you down is a good thing. Calling them out by name is even better.

WHAT'S BEATING YOU DOWN?

It's easy to think negatively or like a "loser." The self-loathing exposed above doesn't grow out of nothing. The number of negative inputs we receive in a single day can hold down the most capable people. I believe these negative messages come at us in the form of four mental bullies. These are who they are and how they impact us.

1. Sensational Media "If it bleeds, it leads" has been a phrase associated with yellow journalism for years. Shock headlines have become the staple diet fed to us by the media and what we're hungry for. In a 1989 *New York* magazine article, staff writer Eric Pooley wrote, "The thoughtful report is buried because sensational stories must launch the broadcast: If it bleeds, it leads."[2] Pooley is widely credited with coining the unspoken motto of TV newsrooms. Marketing trauma is lucrative for the media but damaging to our minds. Recent studies have proven how negative news distorts our thinking.[3]

2. FOMO "Fear of missing out" is now common language to describe one of our mental responses to what we view on social media.[4] We can be fully aware of the reality that what's posted isn't real and still get derailed by envy or feeling left behind. Hearing stories of adventure and joy from a friend is one thing, but to believe everyone has better experiences than you is tough to take. No matter how cognizant we are that what we see are highlight reels, we can feel as if we've missed out on something or that we are just missing life all together. We start thinking lies.

3. Friends and Family This is more than a calling plan. Friends and family can have the most positive impact on our lives, and conversely, the most negative impact on our lives. Elizabeth Dorrance Hall, PhD, has provided practical insights as to why the words of friends and family can be so painful.[5] Here's a quick overview: There's a cultural belief that friends and family will be with us through thick and thin. Our families and friends have a deep well of experiences and observations from our life to draw from. We tend to lean and rely on friends and family for support.

4. Satan and Demons Satan is not only real, he is ruthless! He has demonic forces, and the battle is focused on getting us to think toxically. Shame, unbelief, and blame are a few of the most toxic ways of thinking. Peter warned us, "Be sober-minded; be watchful. Your adversary the devil prowls around like a roaring lion, seeking someone to devour" (1 Peter 5:8). The "roaring lion" metaphor wasn't for dramatic effect. Satan goes after those who are walking away from the security of God through unbelief, rebellion, or deception. But don't look for blatant manifestations of Satan. His best work is done in the shadows, just on the edge of light. If Satan can find an unguarded mind to plant a little temptation, accusation, condemnation, and intimidation, he's got you where he wants you—the bully wins the day. But today is a new day.

Dealing with these bullies is what this resolution is all about. Setting and resetting our thinking is vital for abundant life. I actually have to reset my own thinking several times a day or my mind drifts into toxic territory. Here is a foundational passage about thinking truth that will help you reset:

> If then you have been raised with Christ, seek the things that are above, where Christ is, seated at the right hand of God. **Set your minds on things that are above, not on things that are on earth.** For you have died, and your life is hidden with Christ in God. When Christ who is your life appears, then you also will appear with him in glory. (Col. 3:1–4)

Paul isn't asking us to become irrelevant and disconnected from this world. The opposite is true. The way we stay radiant and contagious is to get all the information we need about the world but receive our identification and direction from God.

We can't afford to get sucked into a losing mindset because it directs our life. The cause and effect of our thoughts and their direct impact on our lives are undeniable. There is no time to waste on this one. Deal a blow to the bullies; it's time to think like a winner.

THINK LIKE A WINNER—BECAUSE YOU ARE!

What you think about today will be lived out in your life tomorrow. It is critical to understand who you are in Christ. If you have come to grips with your sin, confessed it to God, fully surrendered your life to Jesus, and are being led by the Spirit, you are rich beyond imagination. The real challenge is getting rid of a destructive or "losing" mindset.

In the second home my wife and I purchased, the bathroom wallpaper was really out of style. Junanne told me, "Bub (my nickname), the wallpaper has to go." I agreed. But we got busy with life and got used to the wallpaper, so it stayed up for years, and every guest that used that bathroom saw how hideous it was.

If I walked into your mind, what wallpaper would I see? We have messages wallpapering our minds, and if they're not aligned with the truth of God's words, they're going to conceal the truth of His promises. What are the words on your mind? Are they self-loathing, like "fool, failure, mistake, loser, broken, or damaged"? Or maybe they're self-elevating, like "I got it, glad I'm not them, what's in it for me?" Either way, it's got to change.

Junanne loves to tell women she mentors to "wallpaper your mind with truth." But then she helps them do it. I began to hear it so much I started using the process as well. Dr. Caroline Leaf captures the idea this way: "When you objectively observe your thinking with the view to capturing rogue thoughts, you in effect direct your attention to stop the negative impact and rewire healthy new circuits into your brain."[6] In this resolution, I'll give you simple steps to strip the lies off the walls of your mind and put the truth up.

Let's first get a solid standard for right thinking—some good-looking wallpaper. You deserve to know your true identity. Jesus died for you to be free from lies and think truth. Knowing who you are "in Christ" is the most fantastic truth you can internalize. If you have surrendered your life to Jesus and received His grace and forgiveness, you have become a new person.

It's never one-and-done in your battle to think truth. It's a lifetime discipline, with plenty of challenges but a vast reward. Everything about your life flows from thinking rightly about who you are. The most joyful and fruitful people I know still need to regularly revisit the truths listed below. Read these slowly and soak them up.

- I am loved as much as anyone has ever been loved. (1 John 4:10)
- I am officially one of God's kids. (John 1:12)
- I am chosen by God. (John 15:16)
- I am inseparable from God. (1 Cor. 6:17)
- I am carrying the life of God inside me. (1 Cor. 6:19)
- I am a vital member of God's bigger family. (1 Cor. 12:27)
- I am identified by God as a saint, not a sinner. (1 Cor. 1:2)
- I am free from any and all condemnation. (Rom. 8:1)
- I am a brand new creation. (2 Cor. 5:17)
- I am sealed and secured by the Holy Spirit. (2 Cor. 1:22)
- I can go straight to God with anything. (John 16:26–27)
- I am able to receive wisdom for any trial. (James 1:5)
- I am absolutely inseparable from God's love. (Rom. 8:38–39)

God doesn't just love us. We're accepted, changed, and made whole—spiritual winners in the most significant way. In their book *The Cure,* authors John Lynch, Bruce McNicol, and Bill Thrall explain how this acceptance is dependent on one thing alone: "This life in Christ is not about what I can do to make myself worthy of His acceptance, but about daily trusting what He has done to make me worthy of His acceptance."[7]

The Bible's sixty-six books are chock-full of liberating truth—how much God loves us, who we are in Christ, and what we now have in the Holy Spirit. The above are just a few of the high points. But imagine what it would be like to have these truths be an active part of your daily thinking. It can and must happen. Here's how.

BURN IT

His hands were wrapped around a warm cup of coffee, but wrong thinking had a grip on his life. We met at a Starbucks to discuss where Stan was in life. What he was feeling is all too common. Stan felt like a failure as a husband, dad, realtor, and friend. Satan was succeeding in stealing life from him. His once vibrant faith was ice cold. Stan had lost all confidence and didn't want to live. He needed more from me than a shot of inspiration. There was no single verse of Scripture that would be a magic bullet for the harassment he felt at a soul level. Stan needed to get to work—the first step was to think the truth and get the lies out.

I listened to God and prayed what was on my heart for Stan. Then I pulled out a blank sheet of paper from my messenger bag. The exercise I was about to do with him works so well and is so simple that you can pull it off almost anywhere. I asked Stan if he'd be willing to write down everything he was thinking about himself that was troubling or negative. My only promise was that we'd deal with every thought he had; his work was to be brutally honest.

Stan went to work. In ten minutes, he had filled three-quarters of the sheet of paper. It had all the descriptions of shame and anger you can imagine: sadness, embarrassment, pain, frustration, loneliness, apathy, futility—all words a self-loathing person thinks about themselves. There were hints of anger and pride in the mix as well. After I told him to prayerfully search his heart for any more thoughts hiding in deep corners, he wrote a couple more and was done.

I then pulled out one other sheet of paper that included the bullet list from the "Think Like a Winner" section. (On the resource page at the back of the book, you'll learn how to get easy access to this list, digital or hard copy.) I asked Stan to read those biblical truths aloud so that they would become real to him. Below the list, I drew a line down the middle of the blank half of the paper. At the top of the left column, I wrote "Lies to Reject." At the top of the right column, I wrote "Truth to Own." Drawing from all the negative things he'd written about himself on the first sheet of paper, Stan filled in the two columns.

The Truth to Own would be resolved in other meetings. Most of Stan's "truth to own" was sin that needed to be killed. That's why Resolution 3, Kill Sin, is so critical and yet often neglected as you'll see in the next chapter. There's truth to own in your life as well. Let's say you're feeling like a loser because you've been lazy of late. You're not a loser because of who you are in Christ, but you might be "losing" in Redeem Time, the seventh resolution. All of the truths we need to own and take responsibility for will be overcome as we lean into God's grace and power.

But for Stan, those Lies to Reject had to be dealt with . . . and they do with you. The lies to reject are all those thoughts you have that are contrary to your true identity and who you are in Christ. You may have suffered loss, but you're not a loser. You might have behaved in less than lovely ways, but you're not unlovable. You could have slid back into a destructive habit, but you're still a new creation in Christ.

I then surprised Stan with a ceremony. We stepped outside, walked down the street a mile, and sat down on the beach with the Pacific Ocean stretching out before us. Stan tore the Lies to Reject from the sheet of paper and held it in his hand. I joined Stan in a prayer of renouncing these as the paper flapped in the breeze. Then I pulled out a lighter. Stan was now coming to life. We burned those lies as a spiritual ceremony. Satan was put on notice, and Stan felt like he had a fresh start. After cleaning up the ashes, I mapped out for Stan what his next moves would be. They are coming your way as well, in the following five resolutions.

I've asked thousands of people to do this same exercise. This is how discipleship moves from theory to practice. Many experience a deep sense of victory. Maintaining that victory is critical and doable. Here's how.

APPLICATION:
How to Think Truth

MAKE A LIST – On a blank sheet of paper, list everything you're thinking about yourself that is troubling or negative. Be as thorough as possible. Ideally, do this exercise with a trusted friend.

READ THE TRUTH – Read and internalize the bullet list of biblical truths. Don't move through this too quickly. Reading the items aloud will help firmly plant them in your mind. Reread as often as necessary.

SPLIT THE LIST IN TWO – It's time to separate the list of what you're feeling or thinking into two columns. With a fresh sheet of paper, draw a line down the center. Write "Lies to

Reject" on the top of the left column and "Truth to Own" on the top of the right column. Ask God to help you know what negative thoughts go where.

HOLD ON TO THE TRUTH – Tear the list in two. Save the "Truth to Own" column for reference in the following resolutions. God will deal with that as well.

BURN THE LIES – It's time for a ceremony of renunciation. Find a safe place to light the paper on fire. As you burn the list of lies, be sure to agree with God about who you are and that these lies are not it. Enjoy this ceremony.

REHEARSE THE TRUTH – Read the list of truths morning and evening until your mind is wallpapered with the truth. Continue to repeat this process as needed! I do this several times a year myself. It clears my head of lies and gives me actionable truth I need to own—leaning into God's training grace.

Chapter 6

RESOLUTION #3
KILL SIN

◊

Be killing sin, or it will be killing you.[1]

John Owen

I lied to get into Bible college. As I clipped along filling out the application for Multnomah University, I ran into a problem. Staring me in the face was this question: "Do you use any tobacco products?"

Now I was at a crisis point. My integrity was on the line. The question was straightforward, but I figured it would be a deal-breaker if I told the truth. So, with a mouth full of Skoal, I checked the "No" box.

I rationalized my decision. I'd been freed from cocaine and alcohol abuse. God's power and grace had been seen in my life quite demonstrably. I thought a pinch of tobacco here and there was no big deal compared with the sin God had liberated me from a year prior. Truthfully, I chewed Skoal for breakfast, lunch, and dinner, and checking that "No" box was a lie. Skoal had a hold on me, and now I was hiding it.

The decision letter came from Multnomah University a couple of months later—I'd been accepted. I was thrilled to hear the news, but a bit of the shine was off the moment. I had tried to hide my failings to preserve my reputation and pursuits, and now my joy and confidence in Christ were taking a hit. I was feeling like a failure and getting mocked by Satan all at the same time. Now was my moment for reaping the harvest of burying sin—not believing that God had the power to deal with it and underestimating the freedom of bringing it into the light.

When the day came for me to head north on Interstate 5 for Multnomah and the cold, wet weather of Portland, Oregon, I should have been elated, but I was tasting defeat. God had radically cleaned up my life, and yet I couldn't even be trusted to answer a personal question on a college application honestly. Thinking rightly about who I was in Christ was gone because one area of my life was buried and clouding all the rest. That's what sin does when it's covered up, shined up, or simply ignored. I was entering into a cycle of sin, sorrow, guilt, and shame. What would free me from this sin?

As I crossed from sunny, warm California into rainy, chilly Oregon, my shame rose to a fever pitch. In a moment of disgust, I rolled down the window, spitting out the wad between my cheek and gum and tossing out my last can of Skoal. I watched it bounce down the highway and into the long grass on the I-5 median. It felt great! With fresh resolve, I sang aloud along with my favorite tunes, glad to be free of my chewing habit, finally. Surely things were going to be fine now. I may have lied on my application, but I was breaking free.

For another twenty miles, I was on top of the world. I was finished with tobacco. Then it hit me. Overcome with my need for just one more dip, I bolted off at the next exit and headed back to find the can I'd tossed out my car window. On the side of I-5, I parked my car and ran to the median, searching through the tall weeds for just one more dip of chew. After a few minutes, I gave up and trudged back to my car. I was shrouded in shame and felt like an iron curtain now separated me from God. I sobbed over my sin and my apparent inability to kill it.

The lessons learned in the next few weeks would show me the keys to walking free from any sin I faced . . . or that you face as well. I know what you're thinking: "You don't know the power of this sin and how long it's held me captive." I don't care how bad you think it is. No sin can stay standing when faced with God's truth and power for walking free—NOTHING!

WHY YOUR PRAYERS GO NOWHERE

Studies reveal a staggering number of Christians losing the struggle with pornography[2], materialism, and other empty systems.[3] It's sad and hard to admit—we're getting killed by the very things we claim to hate.

This will be tough to hear, but the weight of this truth will make you stronger if you let it. Have you ever felt like your prayers went nowhere? Whether you've thought it or not, your sin can cause God to freeze you out.

Any healthy parent knows how this works. I had to freeze my son's funds one day. We headed out on a big road trip, and Junanne let me know that our son was giving her fits and wouldn't listen to her. I broke the bad news to him: even though he had his heart set on some sports magazines, he wasn't going to have the funds to purchase them until he got his attitude squared away. I froze his funds, and that truth began to sink in. Soon he started listening and honoring his mom. You got it; I unfroze the funds, and he had a great trip.

God loves you enough to get your attention through His silence. Never does God want you to be freaked out over your sin. Sin happens and needs to be confessed and moved on from without much fanfare. If you have brought your struggle into the light and you are engaged with God for resolution, you are never rejected or frozen out. But God does care enough to freeze us out when we allow sin to get a grip on us, and we ignore it or justify it. God wants to get your attention. God is jealous for you to encounter His best, and He won't let you settle for less.

But love compels God to go silent at times. He is unwilling to leave us stunted in growth. Our prayers go nowhere when God wants us to thrive. Are you in a hollow place? Consider the following Scriptures and how they speak to God's love. Own any of these that relate to sin in your life. Hold on to the truth, and don't look away. Freedom is just down the road a bit.

- ***Resisting the Truth*** "If one turns away his ear from hearing the law, even his prayer is an abomination." (Prov. 28:9)
- ***Praying Self-Focused Prayers*** "You ask and do not receive, because you ask wrongly, to spend it on your passions." (James 4:3)
- ***Treating Wives Poorly*** "Likewise, husbands, live with your wives in an understanding way, showing honor to the woman as the weaker vessel, since they are heirs with you of the grace of life, so that your prayers may not be hindered." (1 Peter 3:7)

- ***Practicing Empty Religion*** "'Why have we fasted, and you see it not? Why have we humbled ourselves, and you take no knowledge of it?' Behold, in the day of your fast you seek your own pleasure, and oppress all your workers. Behold, you fast only to quarrel and to fight and to hit with a wicked fist. Fasting like yours this day will not make your voice to be heard on high." (Isa. 58:3-4)
- ***Hiding Your Sin*** "If I had cherished iniquity in my heart, the Lord would not have listened. But truly God has listened; he has attended to the voice of my prayer." (Ps. 66:18–19)
- ***Walking the Fence*** "If any of you lacks wisdom, let him ask God, who gives generously to all without reproach, and it will be given him. But let him ask in faith, with no doubting, for the one who doubts is like a wave of the sea that is driven and tossed by the wind. For that person must not suppose that he will receive anything from the Lord; he is a double-minded man, unstable in all his ways." (James 1:5–8)

When you feel the actual weight of your sin, you are ready to deal with your sin. Sometimes the lack of joy and passion for fellowship with other Christians and any general malaise can be attributed to sin that hasn't been dealt with. Know this for sure: just because God is freezing you out doesn't mean He's mad at you. NO, it's God's love that drives Him to be a wise, functional Father who will get your attention most practically: keeping you from hearing His voice so He can get your life aligned again with truth and His blessings.

Remember the right column from the application of the second resolution—Think Truth? There is "truth to own." The most courageous thing we can do is face our sin and own it. This is the most liberating discipline of the abundant life and practice of every person who has a life that counts deeply.

> WITHOUT THE HATING OF EVIL AND SIN, WE DIMINISH OUR ABILITY TO LOVE.

DON'T YOU HATE THAT?

Hate is not commonly seen as a virtue, but it needs to be. There are things God absolutely hates. Proverbs 6:16–19: "There are six things that the Lord hates, seven that are an abomination to him: haughty eyes, a lying tongue, and hands that shed innocent blood, a heart that devises wicked plans, feet that make haste to run to evil, a false witness who breathes out lies, and one who sows discord among brothers." Romans 12:9 tells us to hate or "abhor what is evil." Hate is the precursor to "hold fast to what is good" (v. 9). Without the hating of evil and sin, we diminish our ability to love. Love without a sharp contrast of what we need to hate just dulls the definition of love and our passion for love. For us to "let love be genuine" (v.9), we need to hate some things deeply.

Knowing exactly what you're hating is critical. The biblical term "sin" is derived from the word *hamartia* in Greek or the word *hata* in Hebrew, which are archery or spear-throwing terms for "to miss the mark" or "flawed." Someone "hamartia-ed" when they did not hit the middle of a target.[4] Cultivating distaste for anything in our life that's missing the mark is virtuous.

Hating sin helps us deal a blow to corruption in our own lives. Think about that sin that you've tried to manage. Impossible, isn't it?

Instead of winking at it, ignoring it, or dumbing it down, hate it. We don't like holding on to what we hate, so give it a go and hate away.

KILL IT

What would it be like for you to beat sin? To get a win over that one area of your life that keeps holding every part of you down? I know you have moments of deep personal resolve and confidence that sound like, "I'm going to beat it this time." But then it's back again—sometimes with more force than before.

Matt and I dueled like there was no tomorrow. From the day my dad popped for some quality table tennis equipment, my best buddy and I couldn't run home from the bus stop quick enough. Raiding Mom's cookie jar and grabbing a glass of milk, we would head to the basement. There, battles ensued as the winter months went by, the number of practice hours piled high. Matt and I were getting good at table tennis.

There was never a time we played that sweat wasn't beading up on our foreheads. We were so evenly matched that to volley the ball back and forth could last for what felt like forever. The only way to win a point was through an unforced error or if the other guy just got too tired. But a moment came when we realized how to stop the volley shorter and score more quickly. We needed to learn and master the "kill shot." The kill shot is defined as: "a decisive smashing or punching of a ball with the hand or a racquet such that it is virtually unreturnable."[5]

Matt and I didn't have to go back and forth once we learned to look for that moment to stop a long volley with a single shot and win a point. The kill shot is the only way to consistently win at table tennis because good players make very few unforced errors, and no matter how tired, few people are willing to give up a point.

Sin is being offered up to us constantly, and we go back and forth in a long volley. We may knock it away from us, but sometimes a specific sin keeps coming back into our court—sometimes sin wins. And sometimes, if we dare to admit it, we're losing the game.

I'm not suggesting that perfection is the goal or even possible—it's not. But sin does not need to define you nor consume you. Sin is exhausting, especially when you're battling in secret, and you see no way to get a win. You can't hide it, deny it, or play with it another day. You have to kill sin, and this is not some term unique to me. God invented the idea of dealing with sin by putting it to death. God's Word indicates that dealing with sin is like a bloody battle—something has to die.

- "Put to death therefore what is earthly in you: sexual immorality, impurity, passion, evil desire, and covetousness, which is idolatry." (Col. 3:5)
- "So you also must consider yourselves dead to sin and alive to God in Christ Jesus. Let not sin therefore reign in your mortal body, to make you obey its passions." (Rom. 6:11–12)
- "And if your foot causes you to sin, cut it off. It is better for you to enter life lame than with two feet to be thrown into hell. And if your eye causes you to sin, tear it out." (Mark 9:45–47a)
- "For if you live according to the flesh you will die, but if by the Spirit you put to death the deeds of the body, you will live." (Rom. 8:13)

Killing sin could be the most neglected resolution of all seven. Killing sin is our calling, and this very real battle saturates Scripture. We can't play with sin. It's a high-stakes game of spiritual table tennis. Satan is serving up sin on a steady basis. Add to that that our heart is easily deceived into thinking we're winning and we're trying to manage things that are hurting us, and we have a royal battle.

It's more than a game, and someone always gets hurt. Don't let it be you. If you feel like you're on the losing end of sin, and shame has you hiding out in the basement of life, know that God sees, cares, and has a plan for you to win . . . and the power to pull it off.

EXPOSE IT—ATTACK IT—OVERWHELM IT

Bring to mind the ugliest sins that have a hold of you right now. Look those nasty things in the face and own how much power they have wielded in your life. God set me free from Skoal addiction, and He kills sin in my life today in the same fashion.

When I say bring your worst, I'm not hedging on the "dark sins," "familial sins," or "lifelong sins." Bring them all: evil thoughts, sexual immorality, stealing, murder, adultery, coveting, pornography, alcohol, prescription drugs, pot, deceit, sensuality, racism, envy, slander, food, spiritual pride, gossip, bitterness, rudeness, boastfulness, and a slew more.

Now let me tell you where we're going with these painful sins. There are three weapons for killing sin. Wield them with spiritual enthusiasm, and I'm fully confident that the sin that has you by the throat today will be under God's foot tomorrow. Here's the biblical approach, and it works:

1. Expose it.

2. Attack it.

3. Overwhelm it.

EXPOSE IT

Bring it into the light of truth by confessing it to God and friends. When you bring sin into the light of truth, three powerful things happen. 1. The cleansing process begins and it's thorough. 2. You realize you're not alone/not the only one. 3. You live in authentic community and are freed from shame and isolation.

Look at the powerful effect of the confession of sin—exposing it gives us a new connection with God and people.

> But if we walk in the light, as he is in the light, we have fellowship with one another, and the blood of Jesus his Son cleanses us from all sin. If we say we have no sin, we deceive ourselves, and the truth is not in us. If we confess our sins, he is faithful and just to forgive us our sins and to cleanse us from all unrighteousness. (1 John 1:7–9)

> Therefore, confess your sins to one another and pray for one another, that you may be healed. (James 5:16a)

Exposing our sin to God and others is the first step of victory over sin. (The fourth resolution will delineate what friends look like and how to find them.) Finding trusted friends who can shoulder with you the sin you're battling is vital for abundant living.

You can take a small step right now. In just a few words, tell God what sin or sins have a grip on you. He knows already, but authentic faith is relational, and your proximity to God will be tighter as the result of your coming clean. There is no need to hang your head. I ask people I pray with to lift their head to God when exposing their sin, and I do it myself. There is something powerful about the symbolism of looking to God rather than hanging your head. Remember, your resolution to Think Right is best applied by killing sin. You have never been more loved, and nothing can separate you from His love. PERIOD!

ATTACK IT

Take extreme measures to put to death whatever sins are killing you. This is where blood needs to be spilled. But, as John Piper explains, there's only one way to prepare for battle. "Until you **believe** that life is war—that the stakes are your soul—you will probably just play at Christianity with no blood-earnestness and no vigilance and no passion and no wartime mindset"[6] (emphasis mine).

This is war, and Jesus got graphic in defining it:

> And if your hand or your foot causes you to sin, cut it off and throw it away. It is better for you to enter life crippled or lame than with two hands or two feet to be thrown into the eternal fire. And if your eye causes you to sin, tear it out and throw it away. It is better for you to enter life with one eye than with two eyes to be thrown into the hell of fire.
> (Matt. 18:8–9)

Jesus is not being literal. He's using hyperbole to make a crucial point: attacking sin at the source is necessary. Killing sin might not be a common topic in conversation, but it needs to be. We discuss sin, find accountability for sin, get counseling for sin, and deal with sin in ways that end up leaving the sin intact and us in pieces. Exploring and being held accountable or even getting counsel around you is fantastic. But all of this needs to come to the "Y" in the road of deciding to put sin to death and finding a strategy for how to do it.

This isn't as tough as you may think. Let me give you an example of how I help men who are honest about their struggle with pornography. This approach of attacking pornography addiction can be applied to any sin that needs to be killed.

Attack the supply line of pornography and make it difficult to access. Technology has exacerbated the problem and placed the bait just a click away. The uptick in the use of pornography is due mainly to its accessibility.[7] It used to be that you'd have to go to a store, a friend's home, or someone else's stash. Now porn is available in an instant.

So I have men come to me with porn problems. It's an epidemic.[8] But the line of attack is simple. Kill your ability to get your eyes on porn.

To start, we take every electronic piece of equipment they own, and I help them create access limits during the times of day or days of the week they have been susceptible to moral failure. Only two trusted allies have the "screen time" and "install" passcodes. We check up in a week. If the supply lines are holding, we celebrate, and if they're failing, we tighten down the limits.

If necessary, I'll help men turn smartphones into dumbphones and the highest-powered laptops into strictly workspaces that allow only texting, emailing, calling, calendaring, and a directional app; that's about it. You can attack supply lines without impeding your life as a student, worker, dad, mom, employer, and friend. And as you'll discover in resolution seven, a ton of this time that had been swallowed up by sin and shame can now be redeemed for God's glory and your good.

Here's the excellent news. Because pornographic images are primarily digital, if you can attack the supply line, you'll have a great shot at victory over all porn. You may need to set limits on your TV as well. Most are smart TVs that can lock kids, or adults, out of channels you don't want to head down.

This is a super plan for preemptive strikes as well. In Proverbs 7, we find the story of a young man who got involved with a married woman—reaping all the short-lived moments of satisfaction. Early in the story, we see that he took the path toward her home. That's where the battle was lost. He should never have gone down that path. It was too much pressure. Cutting off the path to sin usually prevents us from walking into sin. You can do this. Preemptive strikes actually work.

CUTTING OFF THE PATH TO SIN USUALLY PREVENTS US FROM WALKING INTO SIN.

For anything that's killing you and needs to be killed, apply this same approach. If you have a credit card weakness, leave it home, cut it in half, or melt it, but don't have it handy. Ever! If you're trying to curb your appetite, get healthy, or lose weight, don't have the kinds of foods in your kitchen that tempt you to overindulge. If wine, beer, the stiff stuff, or other drugs are owning you, get them out of easy reach, and find those trigger points or trigger people and remove them as much as possible. If social media is devouring your time, put limits on your electronics for this as well.

If you're struggling with people-pleasing, jealousy, ungratefulness, pride, or self-righteousness, there are ways to put these to death. Now let me share a decision one man made to deal with his habitual lying. He was so convicted by God that what was coming out of his mouth was inflated or twisted that he resolved to kill his lying sin by confessing it immediately. If he told a half-truth, he'd stop and say, "That's not the truth, this is what happened as I can best recall." If he spoke a lie and time had elapsed since he did, he'd call that person and tell them that he had lied. In time he killed the sin of lying. You can kill sin too!

Having the right friends is a strategic piece to make this happen. (Resolution 4 will help you find friends who can help you get a win.) With God's grace, courage, and the right support, you can put anything to death that's killing you!

OVERWHELM IT

Your life is finite. We all have a limited number of hours in a day, a certain amount of energy to expend, and capacity limits on friends we can have and money we can spend—life has its limits. It's the same way with sin. If a day in your life is like a fifty-five-gallon drum that contains your day, you have fifty-five gallons of something to put in it. The way to deal with sin is to overwhelm it with the Holy Spirit. The way to kill sin proactively is to fill up (fifty-five gallons if needed) in the Spirit and leave no room for sin. This is exactly what God prescribed.

- But I say, walk by the Spirit, and you will not gratify the desires of the flesh. (Gal. 5:16)
- For if you live according to the flesh you will die, but if by the Spirit you put to death the deeds of the body, you will live. (Rom. 8:13)

Bottom line: Let the Holy Spirit's filling defeat your sin cravings! Sometimes we're so fixated on not sinning we never get on with living. Being filled with the Holy Spirit is about raising the sails of your soul and letting God fill them. It's about saturating yourself with so much good stuff that the bad stuff has no place to grow.

Joining God in spiritual disciplines is the fuel that the Holy Spirit uses to give you anointing and power. The Holy Spirit is God. He is here. He delights in helping you do the most supernatural things possible—overcoming this sin-wrecked world and showing up in heaven hearing, "Well done, my good and faithful servant."

To hear, "well done", we must come alive in the power of the Spirit. The Holy Spirit has been feared, exploited, diminished, de-platformed, and worse, depersonalized. When we are full of the Spirit, we are mindful of what He is saying and doing in our life. The Holy Spirit allows us to starve sin of the attention it so desires.

We can be filled with the Spirit by memorizing liberating truth, singing songs that ignite our soul and lift it, participating in a Bible study that helps us meet with God in His Word, hanging out with people who are on the same path, and being mindful of the Holy Spirit's voice because He is always speaking.

One of my favorite radio interviews was with Asheritah Ciuciu, author of *Full: Food, Jesus, and the Battle for Satisfaction*. In her book, she boils down our need for being filled with God: "At the core, our problem is not really *what* we eat. It's *why* we seek fullness in something that will never satisfy."[9]

Author Asheritah Ciuciu hits too on our need to focus on what can truly satisfy: "Each time we choose God instead of food, our stronghold loses a bit of its power over us. Victory over our enemy takes time, as we repeatedly choose God over anything else that promises to satisfy."[10]

The best spiritual defense is a good offense. If I fill my workplace with words of affirmation, there is less room for a critical spirit. If I fill my stomach with good food, I have less room for junk food. If I fill my heart with hope, my mouth speaks words of encouragement. If I fill my mind with truth, I have less room for believing lies. And if I am filling up with the Spirit, I am bound to starve sin.

APPLICATION:
How to Kill Sin

EXPOSE IT — Bring that sin to mind that needs to die. Courageously face it. Now you have two practical moves to make.

- Confess it to God and come into agreement with Him that you have this in your life and it has to go.
- Call a trusted friend, pastor, or mentor and confess this sin as well to them. Bringing this into the light will bring you unexpected relief.

ATTACK IT — Take extreme measures to kill what's killing you. Remember that limiting access is one of the most practical ways to starve the supply lines of sin.

- Write down a strategy to make this sin less accessible.
- List the people, places, or things that need to be cut off.
- In the fourth resolution, I'll be giving you practical ways to deal with fools in your life.

OVERWHELM IT – It's time to fill your life with the Spirit. Give God more of your life, so sin has less room to run and grow.

- Memorize the promises about faithfulness to God.
- Fill your mouth with songs that produce praise.
- Invite God to read along with you as you're in the Scriptures.
- Listen to the Holy Spirit and keep the conversation going.
- Surround yourself with people who are passionate to kill sin.

Chapter 7

RESOLUTION #4
CHOOSE FRIENDS

◊

The next best thing to being wise oneself is to live in a circle of those who are.[1]

C. S. Lewis

We had just covered a brutal stretch in the Iditarod Trail Sled Dog Race—deep fresh snow, windblown trail, and sixty miles of headwind straight up the mighty frozen Yukon River. It was 1979, and at eighteen years of age, I was halfway through a race of a lifetime. God had blessed me with a whole team of huskies that performed well, but one really had my back. He was the anchor of my dog team. To lose my big wheel dog, Alaska, would be a massive blow to all my dogs and myself.

We arrived at Kaltag in the middle of the night. No one was in sight, so I went searching for a checkpoint manager to mark my arrival. I was standing just inside a nearby house when I heard the screeching and yelps of a dog fight. I ran to my team, but by then, the damage had been done. Some loose village dogs didn't like my team encroaching on their territory, so they attacked. I'm not sure if they went after Alaska, or if he defended the team, but he bore the brunt, and he paid dearly.

I shined my headlamp on Alaska, and his pure white coat was covered with his blood. He looked at me with his piercing blue eyes as if to say, "I defended the team." He did. I picked him up and carried him to a warm shelter and began to tend to his wounds. His hind legs were in the worst shape. Punctured by the other dogs' teeth, his legs oozed fluids, and his muscles twitched when I dabbed at the wounds. I decided to wait for several hours to see if he could heal up enough to get back in harness and go on down the trail with the team. But with time, he only got more stiff. Alaska was done with his Iditarod.

I loaded the final things into the sled and prepared the rest of the team to head for the next checkpoint of Unalakleet. We staked Alaska in an area with the other dogs that had been dropped in Kaltag. As I pulled the snow hook, my team jumped to their feet, and we bolted from Kaltag at a brisk pace after a long break. Within a hundred yards, we passed the dog area where Alaska was staked out. He looked at us with one question in his eyes: "Why are you leaving me, friends?" He couldn't even get to a full-standing position because of his injuries. I wish I could have made him understand why I couldn't take him along.

My sadness was too much; I covered my face with my parka hood and aimed my team for Unalakleet, a hundred miles away, with the command "hike." We were leaving behind the anchor of the team and our good friend. All the dogs and I felt the loss. Oddly, our reunion would be much sooner than I could have imagined.

Traveling the next one hundred miles without Alaska was complicated and made more difficult by even more fresh snow blowing across the trail. I spent several miles walking in front of my team in snowshoes to break open drifted areas that had made the trail disappear. We missed the strength of Alaska, and we all felt his absence. It took me about twenty-four hours to cover that hundred miles. I never saw another team for the rest of the run to Nome, so this stretch helped make us all a little tougher. We would need that to finish the race along a rugged coast.

When we arrived in Unalakleet, I went to a home for some warmth and food. After feeding my team, I went inside to one of the best bowls of chili I'd ever eaten. I was savoring the flavor when we heard a knock at the door. A girl had come to tell me that one of my dogs had broken free. I went outside and counted—all were accounted for. I followed the girl around the corner to the official checker station to try and figure out what she could have meant about "a dog with my team number on its collar."

As I came to the checker station, I couldn't believe my eyes. There was Alaska! As I hugged him, I told the checker, "They must have flown him into town in a smaller plane yesterday while I was on the trail." The checker radioed to Kaltag only to find out that no planes had left town but that "a big white dog had broken free" a day ago.

Alaska had done the unthinkable. His passion for being with me and his team caused him to muster the strength to break free in Kaltag and walk off the injuries as he followed us one hundred miles to Unalakleet. He looked great, and his excitement to have found us was overwhelming.

Race rules didn't allow me to put Alaska back in the team, but after the Iditarod, we were reunited at home and enjoyed many more miles of adventuring through Alaska, the state he was named after. His persistence remains with me to this day as a treasured memory.[2]

How Alaska made it onto my team was a sweet process. I got him from a friend. Over the first few months, we were figuring everything out about each other. As the snow fell and we started to train, I began to see his consistency and commitment to the team. He was strong, but he wasn't a fighter. After many months, I finally *chose* Alaska to make the final cut of my Iditarod team. He had earned this spot with hard work and a great team spirit, proven over thousands of miles in harness. He proved he would add value and be a reliable team member—I was not disappointed.

HAVING FRIENDS IS A FUNDAMENTAL ELEMENT OF ORDINARY LIFE; CHOOSING THE RIGHT FRIENDS IS ESSENTIAL FOR AN ABUNDANT LIFE.

Choosing your friends is a decision you can't take lightly. Having quality people around you who help you live the abundant life is critical. The friends you choose are like an elevator—they can only take you up or down. The race of faith must be run with friends who are going to lift you up and help you "run that you may obtain [the prize]" (1 Cor. 9:24). So much is at stake that we need to choose wisely.

GOOD FRIENDS: THE GAME CHANGER

Having friends is a fundamental element of ordinary life; choosing the right friends is an essential factor for an abundant life. The friends you choose directly impact the choices you make in life.[3] Research also shows that the people closest to us can help, or hurt, our self-control.[4] Even our morality hangs in the balance depending on the friends we choose. "Do not be deceived: 'Bad company ruins good morals'" (1 Cor. 15:33).

There are few things in life that can radically alter the direction of your life like the friends you choose—friends are a game changer. *Game changer* is defined as "a newly introduced element or factor that changes an existing situation or activity in a significant way."[5] More than a fan or an acquaintance, the right friend or friends will stick with you through thick and thin and add value to your life in tangible ways.

> Two are better than one, because they have a good reward for their toil. For if they fall, one will lift up his fellow. But woe to him who is alone when he falls and has not another to lift him up! Again, if two lie together, they keep warm, but how can one keep warm alone? And though a man might prevail against one who is alone, two will withstand him—a threefold cord is not quickly broken. (Eccl. 4:9–12)

THE VALUE OF A FRIEND—THREE OBSERVATIONS

King Solomon masterfully elevated the obvious. He makes at least three wise observations about the value of a true friend that produce one clear conclusion.

1. Multiplied Impact This is one of the most awesome phenomena seen in God's creation. When a person is "going it alone," they possess defined limits of productivity. But add a friend to the equation and now 1+1=3, or possibly more. We can see this in draft horses. Those amazing beasts can pull eight thousand pounds alone. But pair them with another four-hooved friend, and together they pull twenty-four thousand pounds.[6] Amazing! I've seen this with my bride of thirty-four years. When we are locked at the hip around a common goal or task to be done, we energize each other and see that multiplied impact.

A friend who shoulders the load with you is a friend who wants to maximize the potential in both of you.

2. Life Support The question isn't, "Will we fall down in life?" The question is, "Who will be there to help me up?" Football players reach out a hand after being tackled, and a teammate reaches down to help them up. That's basic life support. Mountain climbers take this to the extreme with what's called a "ridge jump." If a climber falls off a high ridge, they need help from the climber roped in with them. To counter the fall and stop them both from falling to their death on one side, the other climber must leap off the opposite side of the ridge to save them both. Now that's life support, and we'll all need it sometime in life.

The "if two lie together" could seem a bit odd unless you know the real need for life support in the harsh elements of winter. I went snow caving for the first time when I was fifteen years old. What an experience. Even though the temperature inside the snow cave is warmer than outside, it is still chilly, as you can imagine. Three of us retained our core body temperature by pressing our sleeping bags close together. It may have looked odd, but we slept safely. Real friends are life support.

A friend who is life support will give up personal comforts and convenience so you can live.

3. Got Your Back This life is a spiritual war, and Satan doesn't fight fair. People don't fight fair either. Defending has to be done from time to time. But having someone who has your back when you're getting bloodied from behind can save your life and help you live to fight another day. Here's the added benefit: when someone has your back, you can venture deeper into enemy territory. Demonic forces are real, they never fight fair, and they come at us from our blind side. Someone who's got your back is a true lifesaver.

A friend who has your back will defend you against gossip, betrayal, misrepresentation, or any number of attacks from your blind side.

Why a Threefold Cord Is So Important

The universal value of the threefold cord is real. When it comes to marriage, business, team sports, adventures, and ministry, having a true friend is critical. Some partnerships fail, but friendships built God's way prevail. So what or who is that third strand?

The third strand is God. The whole context of Solomon's writing is about bringing God into any equation, or it is futile. You need a friend who brings God with them. Engineers know the value of three strands braided together. Each strand becomes more "fault-tolerant" when woven together rather than standing alone. This allows a weak strand to rely on the other two and yet provide strength in other areas. God is the fault-proof strand that holds under any and every circumstance.

A threefold cord is genuinely a game changer. Praying for a friend like this to be part of your life is a noble prayer. Praying that you will be this kind of friend is even better.

IT'S A GOD THING

I used to hurt my brain by trying to grasp that God always was. How could something have always been? I saw puppies born, plants break through the spring soil, and days that brought new challenges, new people, and new adventures—new things were constantly popping up.

J. D. Greear helped jog my thinking about a very important aspect of friendship with the Father, Son, and Holy Spirit. God never created the dynamic partnership of true friendship. Before the very beginning of the beginning, friendship *was*. There was never a time that friendship did not exist.[7] My brain still hurts, but it is true. Friendship is the one thing God never had to create. This is the verse that reveals why.

"Let us make man in our image." (Gen. 1:26a)

FRIENDSHIP WAS NEVER CREATED. IT'S PART OF THE ETERNAL NATURE OF GOD.

The Father, Son, and Holy Spirit were in deep friendship before they made a plan to create the universe or humankind to enjoy it. God created us with the capacity and need for friendship because friendship always was in the very nature of the triune God, and we are made in God's image.

Every relationship or thing we see has a genesis story—a beginning moment in time. Friendship doesn't. Marriage was created because God saw the need. The parent-child relationship was created to fulfill the need for nurturing and growth. Work relationships were created to give us collaboration in subduing the earth and creating new things. But friendship was never created. It's part of the eternal nature of God.

Evil did something that threw a wrench in the works of friendship; we created a relational mess because of our sin. What God designed to be beautiful, we've made awful. Wars are fought, blood is spilled, tears are shed, and grudges linger because we messed it up. So how does God want us to live in this mess?

FOOLS OR FRIENDS: THE CHOICE IS YOURS

Fools bring you down, and friends call you forward. The need to distinguish between them is the difference between life and death. Scripture paints a clear distinction and a beautiful picture of what's possible.

FOOLS I'll just use this one word to describe the folks you should avoid. One of my favorite Scripture passages in all the Bible explains how to move toward a fruitful life. Getting certain people out of your life is not optional.

> Blessed is the man
> who walks not in the counsel of the wicked,
> nor stands in the way of sinners,
> nor sits in the seat of scoffers;
> but his delight is in the law of the LORD,
> and on his law he meditates day and night.
>
> He is like a tree
> planted by streams of water
> that yields its fruit in its season,
> and its leaf does not wither.
> In all that he does, he prospers. (Ps. 1:1–3)

Look at the eye-popping promise—sustainable, fruit-bearing, prospering life. It's better to walk alone for a season with God's Word in your hand than to be in the company of fools, mockers, and scoffers. I'll be sharing with you how to distance yourself from these people.

FRIENDS My wife likes to tell young women that they need a bouquet of friends. I've borrowed this and like to tell men that we need different tools in the chest for different work that needs to be done. Each will add something unique to your life. Indeed, friends are not one-size-fits-all. The sooner we get this, the less frustration we'll have, wanting a friend to do things for us that another friend is wired to do. Peter talks about this very thing.

> Above all, keep loving one another earnestly, since love covers a multitude of sins. Show hospitality to one another without grumbling. As each has received a gift, use it to serve one another, as good stewards of God's varied grace.
> (1 Peter 4:8–10)

Peter lays out clearly that everyone is called to love one another, but how we do that is unique to the gifts God gives us. Unique friendships are what the church is all about. I'm a big believer that engaging in the church is the richest pool to fish in for real friendships. Not everyone who attends church is a potential good friend—resist thinking that the church is a magical place. There are a few weeds mixed in with the wheat. But the best collection of potential friends is in the church. One thing you can do is resist the mentality of "going to church" and start "being the church." Friendships take time to find. But it's worth the work.

NEXT-LEVEL FRIENDS There is another level of friendship that is described in Scripture. These friends are what I call next-level friends. They not only lift you up but also call you forward. Having one or two of these in a lifetime is a true gift from God.

> A man of many companions may come to ruin,
> but there is a friend who sticks closer than a brother.
> (Prov. 18:24)

I've had times when many companions were around me, but I just desired a friend to be with me. Next-level friends are rare, but they can be found. Next-level friends are not perfect, but they have the staying power that average friends can't sustain. I'm going to share with you how to spot a next-level friend, but one thing is most important: live to *be* the friend you so desperately need.

SUCK-UPS AND SURGEONS

There appears to be a significant error in our Bibles. A verse that is so obviously twisted that it just must be a mistake in transcription. "Faithful are the wounds of a friend; profuse are the kisses of an enemy" (Prov. 27:6). Well, nothing is wrong at all. It's a vivid truth about discerning between enemies and friends.

Discerning between suck-ups and surgeons is a challenge, but your eyes will be opened for a lifetime when you get it. Some people present themselves as friends, but they are enemies in friends' clothing. How can you tell the difference? I'll list the contrasts below, but here's the ultimate evidence: an enemy kisses to hurt, and a friend cuts to help. Tim Keller captures it this way: "Like a surgeon, friends cut you in order to heal you."[8] There is nothing as loving as wounds from a friend. When you bring friends along on your journey, you're choosing to befriend a surgeon.

Interestingly, this proverb was written long before Judas's kiss on the cheek of Jesus. Beware of suck-ups. Suck-ups love the benefits of what can be gained, unwilling to pay the price of what true friendship costs. Suck-ups stick with you in the sunshine, but run in the storms. Some "friends" will lavish praise on you while putting a knife in your back.

Here's a chart to compare and contrast how enemies measure up against friends. Keep an eye on the early indicators so you can limit the damage and increase the growth. Remember that the goal is to see yourself become a friend in the most total sense of the word and measure what kind of friend you are.

Enemies (Suck-Ups)	VS.	Friends (Surgeons)
Critical		Hopeful
Betrayer		Confider
Prideful		Humble
Tear Down		Build Up
Kiss to Take		Kiss to Give
Cut to Hurt		Cut to Heal

This may be a tough list to see. It may hit you personally. It might even convict you deeply. But we can't walk away from these truths unchanged. Seeing people as they are is critical to going where God wants to take you. Remember this: enemies always take you down, companions go with you, but true friends pick you up and call you forward.

WHEN THEY SHOW YOU WHO THEY ARE

The most pain I've ever encountered was from true friends. It is beautiful. They tell me the truth; sometimes it hurts, but it ultimately fills my emotional tank to full. They are for me and not against me. These friends have loved me well enough to speak the truth when it cut deeply. But they never leave me to bleed—they are all about health and healing. Having a friend like this is a friend to choose for your walk of faith. They help you run the race. My friends assist me in keeping my eyes fixed on Jesus, "the founder and perfecter of our faith."

Conversely, the most damage I've ever encountered in my life was from "friends" as well. God uses even the most crushing events in life to His glory. No one can avoid getting burned by choosing the wrong friends, but learning early warning signs will help you weed out many who would cost you dearly down the road. Learn this lesson now: when an enemy shows you who they are, believe it!

God is constantly giving us signs in life. The more wisdom we possess, the quicker we see them. Here's my experience with a fool. It's classic in that it is not unique to me. No one has avoided this scenario, and all of us have played this part to some degree in someone else's life.

I was betrayed by him early on. I got a first look at what might happen down the road. There it was. A shot at me behind my back. But he was fun. I enjoyed laughing it up with him, and we had moments of genuine camaraderie. But that first look was a peek at something a wiser man would have seen as a red flag.

Wise counsel warned me to be careful. But I was prideful. My thought was I could handle this relationship. Even though a true friend warned me, I put my opinion above their wisdom. I quickly rationalized the counsel and moved on without a thought of where I was heading and what the cost would be. Never ignore wise counsel when it's offered to you.

"He's undermining you," I was told. When I wasn't around, there were subtle attempts to take my legs out. Statements were made about my character that were untrue or twisted representations of fact. But my modus operandi was "believing the best." But believing the best should never preclude us from accepting the truth. I got busy explaining away the offense and rationalizing his behavior, even to myself. (No one is above correction and being confronted. But Matthew 18 gives us a grid to follow that we must apply: go to the person first before anyone else is brought into play. Based on how that goes, Matthew 18 continues on with the next healthy biblical steps. We need to play by the rules, and you deserve to choose friends who play by the rules.)

Then it was too late. The ultimate damage to myself and others was crushing to me, my family, and many others. The relational shrapnel scarred many. Collateral damage and the lingering effect of relational chaos can be devastating, and we've all experienced it. I have two critical things for you to note: 1. Take an assessment of how you're treating people and especially friends. In any relational damage, there is something you can own. Own any part you played without regard to the other party. God used my pain to bring more order into my life and make me more of a friend others could choose with confidence. 2. Know this for certain: no matter how much pain you've had in friendship and with enemies in friends' clothing, God is the healer. God can take your wounds of relational pain and turn them into sacred scars. You may want to join God in prayer at this moment and let His love touch you deeply.

> THE ONLY THING GREATER THAN CHOOSING FRIENDS IS BEING A FRIEND SOMEONE WANTS TO CHOOSE.

There is a friend out there for you. Jonathan was King Saul's son. He was in line for kingship, but he gave it up for friendship. Jonathan made a covenant of friendship with David that would be passed down to their children. When it became clear that Jonathan's dad was aiming to kill David, Jonathan said these words to his friend in a grassy field: "''The Lord shall be between me and you, and between my offspring and your offspring, forever''" (1 Sam. 20:42b).

Pray for wisdom to find a Jonathan or two in your life. But be the friend you want. Don't surrender to the lesser; seek God to bring you the friend or friends you need. Be intentional. And agree with God to become the very friend you need. The only thing greater than choosing friends is being a friend someone wants to choose. Be the kind of friend you want have.

APPLICATION:
How to Choose Friends

SEPARATE YOURSELF FROM FOOLS – When someone shows you who they are, believe it. God loves fools, but He doesn't expect you to make them your friends. Pray for them, but don't partner with them.

- Realize you don't change people – Don't spend any time trying to make fools into friends. The Holy Spirit does the heavy lifting of true change. We need to love our enemies, but we in no way are called to make fools our friends.

- Distance yourself – Sometimes the best way to love fools and enemies is to distance yourself. It is better to walk alone for a season with just you and God than to get dragged down by fools.

- Special Note – If you find yourself married to a fool or in a partnership with a fool that you can't extricate yourself from, I want to give you some encouragement.

    - First, pray for them to change. Ask God to reveal to them His love and the power of His grace to change them.
    - Second, get some wise counsel from someone who can hear your heart and pray with you. They will provide objectivity and wisdom and point you back to trusting God.
    - Third, guard your heart, and never give them something today that they can use against you tomorrow.
    - Fourth, be humble and introspective. We can overestimate our virtue and underestimate others.

LOOK FOR FRIENDS OF GOD – Many things can pull people together. Hobbies, habits, politics, cuisine, culture, and shared dreams. But the one thing that puts steel in the cement of friendship is God. You've read this far because you want God's promises to be fully realized, and you've resolved to take hold of them.

- Focus on passion for God – Find people who share the same love for God. You're not looking for perfect people but those who are certainly on the same path of following Christ. We can have rich acquaintances with people from other religions or even atheists, and forging those relationships is God's call on His kids. But friendships that have staying power through storms are built on the rock of Jesus Christ.
- Watch how someone responds to adversity – Resist judging yourself by your best intentions, but judging others by a single moment of weakness. Everyone's cup is going to get bumped, and what comes out isn't always pretty. Don't write off everyone who has a moment of weakness, but see if they humbly own it. If they do, you may have found a diamond in the rough.

CHOOSE YOUR FRIENDS INTENTIONALLY – Don't relinquish your right to choose friends. Agree with God that you'll never leave friends to chance or convenience. True friends have more passion for honoring God than self-promotion or approval by man.

- Don't be hasty – Finding true friends takes time. Choosing friends needs to be in the context of life as it really is. Take the time to see someone in the highs and lows of life. Time is always on your side when choosing friends.
- Be open to surprises – Friends often come in packages that may surprise you. God will give us friends who look and act very differently than ourselves. Background and

style are not the measures for choosing friends. Look for those who aim to glorify God and help you win—substance matters more than style.

- Ask them to be your friend – Formalizing friendship is something too few really do.
- Take the time to sit down and affirm your shared convictions, passions, and life direction. Speak out the truths of friendship as outlined in this resolution and commit yourself to being the kind of friend who can be trusted.

Chapter 8

RESOLUTION #5
TAKE RISKS

Life is risk, and risk is right. To run from it is to waste your life.[1]
John Piper

The woman screamed her horrific confession to King Jehoram: "So we boiled my son and ate him" (2 Kings 6:29). Imagine the terror and anguish of being locked in a city with supply lines cut off—no one getting out and no food coming in. Ben-hadad, King of Syria, had the people of Samaria surrounded, and all hope was gone. The people of the city were starving to death, and the unimaginable was happening.

The death toll was rising daily. So hungry were the Jewish citizens of Samaria that a horse's head, deemed unclean by law and inedible in normal conditions, was selling for eighty shekels of silver—over one year's wages. Even two quarts of dove dung were garnering five shekels of silver. The hunger pangs had driven two mothers to do the unthinkable.

Standing high on the city's wall, King Jehoram was now trying to resolve a conflict between two women who stood below. A deal had been struck. The day before, they had killed one woman's son with an agreement to kill the other woman's son the following day. Now the woman whose son had been eaten wailed in pain, shame, and rage that the other woman had hidden her son.

King Jehoram ripped his clothes with no words to speak and collapsed onto a sack made of goat hair. His grief turned to fury, and he called for his men to find Elisha. Since the prophet seemed unable to free the people from the Syrian army's grip, the king wanted Elisha's head on a platter.

Elisha sat in his house with the elders. God gave His prophet a word that a messenger was coming for him. With the door to the home now blocked, Elisha yelled out to the messenger that in twenty-four hours, the city would be thriving, the economy restored, and all would be safe. Elisha's story seemed impossible. The messenger mocked Elisha, "If the Lord himself should make windows in heaven, could this thing be?" Elisha only said, "You shall see it with your own eyes, but you shall not eat of it" (2 Kings 7:2b).

"Now there were four men who were lepers at the entrance to the gate." This turn in the story, found in 2 Kings 7:3, is not a strange subplot. It was God's providential plan for Samaria's liberation about to unfold. The four lepers were done for. Usually, their banishment for a skin disease had them begging for food, but now they waited to die. What could they possibly do?

They took the ultimate risk. Considering their dire situation, the four agreed to walk to the Syrian camp and beg for mercy. They were in a challenging situation. They calculated that if they died at the hands of the Syrians, it would be swift.

But God! As the lepers shuffled in the twilight toward the Syrians, God did what God does. God made their steps to sound like a vast army complete with chariots. The Syrians assumed King Jehoram had contracted with foreign militaries, and in their panic, they ran for their lives.

Imagine the shock when the four lepers walked into the abandoned camp. With horses, tents, donkeys, silver, gold, and all the Syrians' food left behind, they gorged themselves and drank until full. Quickly they remembered the city that had shunned them. Before the sun rose, they arrived at Samaria to share the good news. But their story was not believable. The king believed that a trap had been set, but he sent out a few horses and riders just to see.

Soon word spread that the Syrians were on the run. Those remaining in Samaria who had the strength ran through the gates to plunder the enemy camp. The messenger who mocked Elisha the day before was stampeded to death—he saw the deliverance but never tasted the spoils of victory.

It's one of the most moving stories in the Bible. God chooses four lepers to save a city under siege. It captures the themes of our lives today with drama, scope, and scale we may never understand. But the lessons are for us, and the themes ring through the pages of Scripture and into eternity. God is always aware of our needs; He has the power to save entire cities, and He loves to leverage risk-takers for His glory.

God does some of His most significant work through those who take risks. The Bible has a hall of fame of risk-takers from every walk of life. Right there in Hebrews 11, we see kings, paupers, up and outers, down and outers, princes, and prostitutes—it appears anyone can make it into the hall of fame of risk-takers. And that goes for you!

THE TIME IS NOW

People who say Christians shouldn't take risks have diminished the gospel. The book of Acts is loaded with risk and risk-takers. We have the gospel today because someone took a risk for our sake. It's time to agree with God that faith is an adventure, and you're ready to take a walk. Taking risk is a central theme in deliverance stories, new discoveries, and all of God's promises. Risk-taking is not an invitation to recklessness, ignoring the truth, or rejecting wise counsel. But taking risks is the joy of God's kids who want to walk by faith.

GOD CAN DO MORE IN THE ELEVENTH HOUR THAN YOU CAN DO IN THE TEN PRIOR.

Risk naturally involves a certain level of fear. No matter what you may fear at any given moment, God has supernaturally placed within you a spirit of power, love, and self-control (2 Tim. 1:7). It's never too late, and you're never too old. You're never too worn out or too worn down. You're never too lost or too far gone. You're never too battered and never too shattered for God to pull it all together. God can do more through your frailty than you can ever pull off through all your learning, skills, and strength. If you can take a breath, you have a life that needs to be fully lived. Don't let your dreams die.

God can do more in the eleventh hour than you can do in the ten prior. There's a debilitating lie that roams around boardrooms, is whispered in small groups, and wages a private war against our minds. This lies pushes God-given potential and endless possibility further into a dark hole of discouragement and defeat. And here is the subtle killer: "Past performance is the best predictor of future success" or "your current situation will never change."[2]

These are grand lies. They deny that "we are more than conquerors through him who loved us" (Rom. 8:37). These lies ignore that we can "overcome the world," including what has conquered us in the past. They overlook endless biblical stories of redemption. And these success stories are often built on prior failures. They ignore God's passion for changing lives and His power to do it. They reduce the transformation to a wish and leave Jesus dead in the grave. We can't let the dream die, and the only way forward is to trust God enough to take risks. The time is now.

Imagine the battle a self-educated cobbler would face. It must have been a secret of his heart for some time before he dared to share his dream to reach India's people with the good news of Jesus Christ. This shoemaker risked shame, sharing his passion with a few spiritual leaders. One seasoned pastor called him a "miserable enthusiast" to his face. But the courageous young man held onto his dream, fighting through multiple setbacks and momentary bouts of defeat and taking risks and trusting God.

He pressed on, and the result of the risks he took was not meager. After much learning and years of toil, he translated the Bible into forty languages. He began a university that exists today, and he died seeing the subcontinent of India rocked with the gospel—his dream lives on, and millions of lives have been impacted by the risks he dared to take. His name is William Carey. He is famous for this epic challenge: "Expect great things from God; attempt great things for God."[3]

When we feel frail, God loves to show Himself faithful. Any notion that God paints a general picture of a more abundant future and then abandons us to stumble along is flatly untrue. William Carey leaned into God as he risked what others thought to be fantasy. Nothing gives God more joy than moving you from where you stand today to taking courageous and bold steps tomorrow, and ultimately realizing the promises that He gave you.

THIS IS WAR

Imagine being there when the church in Ephesus opened the letter from Paul. How awesome would it have been to hear Paul's passion that "the eyes of your hearts [be] enlightened," to know "the hope to which he has called you," and to grasp "the immeasurable greatness of his power" (Eph. 1:18–19)—what a vision to pursue. Paul knew this well: any great vision will face opposition. He was beaten, stoned, mocked, and left for dead. But Paul's calling was worth the risk.

You need to know this going in and moving ahead. A certain level of risk is inevitable. The forces aligned against God's kids are strong, but retreat is not an option. We're in a battle.

> Finally, be strong in the Lord and in the strength of his might. Put on the whole armor of God, that you may be able to stand against the schemes of the devil. For we do not wrestle against flesh and blood, but against the rulers, against the authorities, against the cosmic powers over this present darkness, against the spiritual forces of evil in the heavenly places. (Eph. 6:10–12)

I like to highlight one crucial point that's often missed. People are NOT the enemy. Satan may work through people at times, but the driving force of opposition is not flesh and blood—this is a spiritual war.

The minute we get serious about anything in life, we will face resistance from dark spiritual forces. These forces will bombard us and mock us—tempting us to settle for too little. I don't care what risk you take to put your life out there, large or small. Lead discussion groups for at-risk marriages; use a skill to train fatherless boys; eradicate an addiction and print the story for others to read; conquer fear and help your kids overcome it as well; witness to your neighbors and watch your building, and then your block, be transformed by Jesus Christ; begin a business that profits the world and points people to God; or step away from any comfort for the sake of comforting others. Spiritual forces are lurking for anyone who dares to take risks. The enemy is in the air, on the ground, and trying to get in your head.

This is the case in our dreams and desires. I've never met a single person who wanted an adventure with God but didn't experience resistance in challenging and tangible ways: "Indeed, all who desire to live a godly life in Christ Jesus will be persecuted" (2 Tim. 3:12). Godliness is resisted at every turn. Spiritual forces, and those people Satan can enlist, are continuously pressing us to stop dreaming, stop being radical, give up, and never risk failure. The messaging tells us to return to mediocrity because mediocrity loves company. These voices never reveal that all they're selling is giving up on God's best for us, masking it in caution and responsibility.

Battles are unavoidable. They can't be ignored, circumvented, or even put off, but they can be won. The sooner we come to grips with challenges of all kinds and severe spiritual conflict, the sooner we can get on with winning the war. Let's stake claim to solemn spiritual promises right now. God can get us through our battles. In Christ, we prevail. It's time to take a risk.

"GOD, JUST A LITTLE BIGGER THAN ME"

When we take a risk, we place ourselves in a position where faith and trust in God can grow. That's what God did with me when He showed me how much I needed His help in a whiteout on the coast of Alaska.

I was in the middle of the 1,100-mile Iditarod Trail Sled Dog Race in 1979. Young and unafraid, I drove my dog team straight into the teeth of a fierce storm on the Alaska coast. Against the counsel of village elders in Shaktoolik, I headed right into the path of a coastal storm. I was traveling slowly with my eight huskies as the storm grew in intensity. At one point I stepped off the runners of my sled to see how fast we were moving—we were stopped, stalled on the sea ice many miles from shelter or assistance.

In below zero temperatures and winds gusting to ninety miles an hour, I crawled through zero visibility, holding onto the sled and tug lines as I made my way to each dog. To let go for a second in a whiteout could mean a helpless search for my team and crawling to my death. When I reached my dogs, I carefully huddled them together in a big ball to keep them warm. I crawled back to my sled. Putting up a makeshift windscreen around my sled I slid into my sleeping bag with all my gear on, estimating my chances of dying. I called out to God. This was bigger than me, and only He could help me. But did God hear?

Within a few hours, the winds subsided just enough to get my freezing body and weary dogs to get up to try again. At the command, my brave dogs leaned into their harnesses. They knew time was of the essence. I'm alive to tell you about this stretch of the Iditarod today only because of God's grace.

God often takes me back in my mind to that frozen moment in time. He wants me never to forget the secret to Christian adventure and abundant life: we continuously need things in our life that are "just a little bigger than me." In truth, everything is bigger than us, and we only breathe by God's grace and power. But risk-taking puts you in that place of constant dependence.

We do a lot in our power, strength, and ingenuity, never trusting God, only relying on self. But that's not where the jazz and joy of faith are found. The secret has to get out. We have to take risks and engage in a life that we know is bigger than us, or we'll shrink in our apathy and settle for mediocrity.

YOU CAN BELIEVE GOD TO USE YOU SIGNIFICANTLY OR SETTLE FOR SELF-FOCUSED MEDIOCRITY, BUT YOU CAN'T DO BOTH.

Remember the goal: God gets the glory; we get the joy. I just love how Henry Blackaby captured this in *Experiencing the Spirit*.

> Will God ever ask you to do something you're not able to do? The answer is yes—all the time! It *must* be that way, for God's glory and kingdom. If we function according to our ability alone, we get the glory; if we function according to the power of the Spirit within us, God gets the glory. He wants to reveal *Himself* to a watching world.[4]

You can believe God to use you significantly or settle for self-focused mediocrity, but you can't do both. As seen in the lives of four lepers, the smallest risks taken can impact the masses. It's the most counterintuitive prayer you can speak to God, but it holds the most promise: "God, just a little bigger than me."

THE GIANTS ARE STILL THERE

The nation of Israel wandered in spiritual mediocrity for forty years because ten men didn't want to take the risk (see Num. 13:25–33). God's promises for you are like the promised land offered to Israel. The big fruit, rolling hills, and freshwater streams are intermingled with giants that want to oppose you taking the land.

When forty years had passed, Joshua and Caleb finally got their reward. But the risk was the same—the giants were still there. These were not fearless moments. Joshua didn't look across the Jordan and say, "I got this." No way! God told Joshua to be "strong and courageous" because He knew he needed a pep talk and more. God read Joshua's mind. Joshua was thinking, "I don't know if I can do this." This was bigger than Joshua, the perfect risk to take.

There are three real practical moves Joshua made to take hold of God's promise. We all get stuck . . . and probably are stuck in some area of our life even now. Seasoned Jesus followers, new believers, elders, staff, and even lead pastors have something in common. We find ourselves this side of God's promises more often than we'd like to admit. These three actions provide an excellent application for any risks you take to follow God. They are found in the first eight verses of the book of Joshua, chapter 1.

GET UP

Nothing can strike fear into our hearts like leaving what is familiar. As much as we might hate where we are in life, there is a little comfort in what we know, even if the standard is mediocre. So, after all the excitement of dreaming, imagining, planning, and envisioning is done, there comes a time to move. That's when the reality of a given situation sets in. The challenges and opposition become more vivid. The intoxication of a potential new adventure, new life, or a fresh start is sobered up when we hear "get up."

> "Moses my servant is dead. Now therefore **arise**, go over this Jordan, you and all this people, into the land that I am giving to them, to the people of Israel." (Josh. 1:2)

God called out for Joshua to "arise." This adventure was now getting real. At this moment, Joshua had to face the risk of what lay ahead and agree with God. This first move was critical for Joshua. He had to get up.

When God says "arise," He plainly means for us to stand up or get up.[5] We don't have to wonder if it's God's will or the right time. The moment the Holy Spirit convicts you, it's time to get up, to "arise." It's the grace of God to realize that you've settled for less for too long. And it's the grace of God that will get you unstuck.

Of this, you can be sure: no one is more passionate to see you go after God's best than God Himself. That God-given vision to engage in something that is beyond you but compels you? Get up. That wind of God's Spirit that is moving you toward your ultimate calling—get up and feel it. That big dream that God gave you, and you've maybe never told a soul—get up and never again settle for less than God's best. "'Today, if you hear his voice, do not harden your hearts as in the rebellion'" (Heb. 3:15).

GO OVER

Every one of us has a river in our life. That river stares us down and dares us to take that first big step. Your river stands between you and

God's great promises for your life. It has to be crossed because a river can't be walked around. At times, the river taunts us and tells us to not even make plans for the other side. But make no mistake, your river is crossable by God's grace and power.

Between the mediocrity caused by Israel's lack of faith and the victory ahead flowed a river. God told Joshua one thing: "Go over."

> "Moses my servant is dead. Now therefore arise, **go over** this Jordan, you and all this people, into the land that I am giving to them, to the people of Israel." (Josh. 1:2)

There's a crossing in your life, and it's just ahead. Taking that first big step is often the most challenging—and terrifying—step to take because there are so many unknowns. "Will I make it?" and "will it be worth it?" are just two of the questions that will bombard your mind with fear. But to get on with life, we have to go over a river; we just have to take that first big step.

And if there is a river, plan to get wet. The Jordan was ultimately stopped up, and the river bed wasn't even damp—it was dry. But that came *after* the crossing began. Don't wait for the miracle. Go over.

Launch the business God showed you no matter how big the task appears. Be wise and thoughtful, but step into that tough conversation with your son. Say yes right now to that ministry that will finally utilize your spiritual gifts, no matter how scary it is. Start writing that book. Move to that city that fits you, glorifies God, and gives you joy. Redecorate the bedroom to bring in guests. Leave your job if that's what God said. Begin that workout regime. It could be your river is leading a small group or learning a language. Some are called to "go over," and the river is improving your health, shoring up your finances, painting the picture, or repairing your broken marriage. Some require personal courage like speaking up for yourself or someone you love. And if you need to cross over from busyness into peace, go. Whatever your river, it's time to go over.

God may be showing you what your river is right now. Or maybe it's just a sketchy line on a map that you see. In all the forecasting God gives us, He rarely gives us the details of the plan. That's for one simple reason: the dream God has given us can only be realized through utter dependence. Take that risk and go over.

BE STRONG AND COURAGEOUS

When God told Joshua to "be strong and courageous," He was giving him more than a pep talk. Like every other time God speaks a word of encouragement, it's coupled to something tangible and actionable. Strength and courage in the face of fear and risk are not found in a rallying cry. They're found in something much more powerful. Look at the following narrative with an eye for what lies within God's calling to Joshua.

> "Be strong and courageous, for you shall cause this people to inherit the land that I swore to their fathers to give them. Only be strong and very courageous, **being careful to do according to all the law that Moses my servant commanded you. Do not turn from it to the right hand or to the left, that you may have good success wherever you go. This Book of the Law shall not depart from your mouth, but you shall meditate on it day and night, so that you may be careful to do according to all that is written in it. For then you will make your way prosperous, and then you will have good**

> **success.** Have I not commanded you? Be strong and courageous. Do not be frightened, and do not be dismayed, for the LORD your God is with you wherever you go." (Josh. 1:6–9)

God's call to strength and courage was built on the hope that Joshua would live by the book. God knew this: if Joshua lived by the playbook, penned by God through humans, he would have prosperity and success. There was nothing to fear. Joshua was taking a reasonable risk because God had a plan, and all Joshua had to do was follow it.

If you listen closely, you can hear God's voice cheering you on. But the cheering isn't half-baked or based on nothing. God invites us to take risks while we hold tightly to His promises and the truth that makes those promises possible. It's the Word of God that enables us to navigate risky situations and come out the other end with victory. All risk-taking must never let go of what God is saying. Risk-takers are Bible readers. Risk-takers are truth talkers. Risk-takers revere God's Word more than flying by the seat of their pants or walking in their wisdom.

APPLICATION:
How to Take Risks

GET UP – There is too much at stake to settle for less than God's best another day.

- Get up! I mean physically. Stand up and tell God (aloud), "I will not settle for too little. I will take risks with my life. Your Word will be my guide."
- Repeat it several times and with increasing volume. Put some punch behind it until you're on the edge of ridiculous.
- Repeat as often as necessary, and then add one more for good measure. It's time to get up.

GO OVER – The river will not go away. It may dry up, God might send rafts, but you have to cross it. It's time to go over! So what is it? That river you face has a name. There may be many names. Name it and cross it.

- Write down the name of the river. All the names that come to mind, write them down. It could be a person, place, or thing.
- Be specific with the action needed. Is it launching, speaking up, leading, improving, learning, shoring up, repairing, or even giving up? Whatever this river represents for you, it's likely an action step you need to take in order to set yourself up for risky obedience to God.

- Tell a trusted friend the river(s) you need to cross. Also let them know the tangible actions needed. Whatever your river, it's time to "go over."

BE STRONG AND COURAGEOUS – God is speaking to you, and He is confident you can fulfill His calling. His confidence is based on His precepts. God's truth is what makes Him confident that the risks you take are measured and responsible. This is what you must do.

- Agree with God that His Word will be a central part of your life. More than a token nod to God, you'll be a person of the Word.
- Agree with the Holy Spirit for guidance in the Word.
- Embrace the benefit of a local church to help you live out God's Word in your life.
- When you fail to take the time to hear God's voice and counsel, get back up and dig into God's Word again.
- With God's Word hidden in your heart, be strong and courageous as you step out and take risks.

Chapter 9

RESOLUTION #6
FOCUS EFFORT

A person who aims at nothing is sure to hit it.

Anonymous

"The score takes care of itself." That's a philosophy as well as the intriguing title of the book by coaching legend Bill Walsh.[1] The fact that the book is about a man who changed the way his game was played and that his approach bred winning, winners, and a stable of winning coaches and teams? I was all in.

You don't have to be a football fan to appreciate what Walsh did for the game. As the head coach of the San Francisco 49ers, Walsh struck on God's vision for excelling that many pastors could learn from. He was tempted to quit before he could get his philosophy off the ground. It's a good thing for all of us he didn't quit because his approach is timeless and transcendent whether he knew it or not.

Walsh inherited a team that went 2–14 the prior season. He did no better than his predecessor in his first year. By the end of the second year, he had a combined record of 8–24. Some wondered why he never talked up pursuing Division and Championship titles. This is the genius of Bill Walsh. He resisted setting lofty goals and opted for empowering players to find their fit and excel at their position.

> I had no grandiose plan or timetable for winning a championship, but rather a comprehensive standard and plan for installing a level of proficiency—competency—at which our production level would become higher in all areas, both on and off the field, than that of our opponents. Beyond that, I had faith that the score would take care of itself.[2]

This is much like God who tells us to find our gifts and use them. He doesn't say specifically what will come of it, just to get using them, and we'll all be the better for it (Rom. 12; 1 Cor. 12). The following season, the 49ers went on to win their first Super Bowl under Coach Walsh. He changed the style of play from grinding it out by running the ball or throwing long bombs as the only option. His "West Coast" offense was built on getting the right person in each position, ensuring sharp execution in those positions, and letting the score take care of itself.

It was a winning strategy that worked on the field, and many found it produced winning in companies. Walsh's legacy rivals any coach in football history, and his unique approach to winning has shaped entrepreneurs, CEOs, and leaders around the globe.

STOP SETTING GOALS!

I can hardly believe I got myself to write the title of this section. I've done goal setting for most of my adult life. But everything changed about ten years ago. Maybe I'm a slow learner, but I saw over time that what matters most is not lofty goals but a rigorous consistency of executing the right things in my daily life. These things are easily discerned and unique to the way God wired me.

Goal setting has some value but not before you know who you are (Resolution #1) and how you are. What I mean by "how you are" is God's unique design of your life—how you are equipped by God with all your passion, gifts, and talents. When you were unfolding in your mother's womb, God was mapping out every one of "the days that were formed" for you (Ps. 139:16).

Our primary aim is joining God, not setting goals. It is to get our life aligned with God's will. We often think we need to develop grand plans for what we'll do or achieve. We see influencers around us and measure our worth or our pursuits up against them. Two errors can happen at this juncture: 1. We keep stacking ourselves up against other people and feel like we fail. 2. We resign ourselves that our life won't count enough, so we leave too many chips on the table.

Goal setting has value, but it's not the most important thing you can do. Knowing your calling and where precisely to focus your effort is far more critical than goal setting. You see this over and over in the Scriptures.

Paul the Apostle

This world shaper had no defined target goals beyond preaching the good news, raising young leaders, and touching base with churches planted to keep them on point. He didn't set a goal for numbers of people in these churches or how many would be planted. He didn't know if he'd survive his first mission excursion, let alone be used to reach the world with the gospel. I'm convinced: Paul's flexibility led to his productivity.

If his goal had been to bust straight North and reach Asia with the gospel, he'd have blown right past the direction of the Holy Spirit and missed reaching Macedonia. He wanted to get to Rome and Corinth so much, he told them in letters. But Paul's mental goals were always submissive to his ultimate calling.

> "But I do not account my life of any value nor as precious to myself, if only I may finish my course and the ministry that I received from the Lord Jesus, to testify to the gospel of the grace of God." (Acts 20:24)

Preaching grace got Paul out of bed in the morning. He didn't care where God put him or who was in front of him. It was all about getting people freed from religious performance and into a relationship with the living God. Paul had the needed passion, necessary gifting, and sensitivity to the Spirit to preach the gospel. The score took care of itself, and the world owes a debt of gratitude to Paul for living his calling one day at a time.

Josiah the King

The poor kid came to power following his dad's assassination. Josiah had zero legacies to look to. His granddad and father had fatal flaws that spelled doom for the young king.

But Josiah did the unthinkable. He hitched his wagon to the life of King David who reigned four hundred years before him. He had learned through oral tradition that David did one thing with his life that brought the blessing Josiah's dad and granddad had missed. Even Luke recounts the life of David as focused on God, who said of David, "'I have found in David the son of Jesse a man after my heart, who will do all my will'" (Acts 13:22). Josiah's mission in life was all about seeking God and getting direction from Him.

> For in the eighth year of his reign, while he was yet a boy, he began to seek the God of David his father, and in the twelfth year he began to purge Judah and Jerusalem of the high places, the Asherim, and the carved and the metal images. (2 Chron. 34:3)

Josiah never stopped! He kept in step with everything God showed him to do. When the lost Torah, absent for two hundred years, was rediscovered, he repented at its reading. His repentant heart, aimed to give glory to God, was so aligned with God that his generation was spared. Only under the next king would Israel be hauled off to captivity in Babylon because they lost focus on God.

Here's the point: Josiah didn't set a goal to be blessed by God and spared captivity. He was more fixated on honoring God with his everyday life than aiming to build a name for himself. In the process, he built a powerful legacy and a strong reputation, and he and his people lived in freedom throughout his life.

Paul, Josiah, and all the great men and women of Scripture have something in common. They excel at knowing who they are and what they're called to be and do. Then they set about repeating the same life-giving actions over and over. They have healthy habits. It's the small things executed daily that produce the most significant and lasting results. But look at what we're up against.

SCATTERED, SMOTHERED, COVERED

My friend had kept hounding me to grab a bite at a Waffle House, so I finally joined him for breakfast at this Southern chain with a huge following. It turns out this place not only has rabid followers, but it also has its own language. If you don't speak Waffle House when you get there, it's a bit of a learning curve.

My friend said he'd order for us. The waitress soon arrived, and words came out of his mouth I'd never heard: "Scattered, smothered, covered." To me it sounded like he was sharing how his life was going. But the waitress knew what those words meant: hash browns flung across the grill, enough onions to choke you, and cheese that brought it all together.

But these words are an excellent descriptor of our life. We are too scattered in our thinking and doing, smothered with endless opportunities and decisions, and covered with guilt or shame when we believe we're not doing enough or we're doing all the wrong things.

I want to cut you some slack. We live in a world that inundates us with options and decisions like no other generation has faced. The problem is just getting worse. Your need to focus your efforts has never been more requisite to having your life count and experiencing peace. Yes, your life can both count for something great and be swept along by the peace of God. But not until you fully grasp what you're up against.

Take a look at the space around you right now. Just the view from where I'm writing in my office reveals how many things, even good things, can leave me scattered, smothered, and covered. In my 6'x10' rooftop getaway, I have bands for resistance training hanging up, a light ring for shooting videos, our family travel itinerary, bills to pay, a honey-do list that keeps growing, and memorabilia from events and achievements. There are goal charts, headphones, smart devices, photo albums, dream boards, chargers for everything, an external microphone, some stuff that looks too important to throw out, and one whole shelf of bestselling books on how to do more with your life.

It's no wonder our minds are scattered and we have little quiet time to process what's happening in our life. We're experiencing information overload like no other time in history.[3] But rather than cutting loose some of the options, we try to manage them. It's not working.

We may be a bit smarter with all these devices, but beyond pure content we have pop-ups, passwords, security questions, apps, more apps, and renewal fees. Just as I was writing this, I was alerted to a duct cleaning special and an offer from my recent DNA home test kit to know even more about my genetic makeup (what I already know is scary enough!). We blindly click "agree" on extensive user agreements because we have no time to actually read them, let alone figure out if we really do agree.

There are good reasons why tech giants put digital content restrictions on their kids.[4] We live in a time when being intentionally disconnected is becoming more vogue than the latest device you can purchase. There's actually a movement called National Day of Unplugging.[5] The accessibility of information is falling in on us. In the crush of information, options, and decisions, it's hard to focus on our God-given passions, gifts, and talents, if we've even had time to discover them in the first place.

Added to all the digital stimulants, we're still battling people-pleasing, and we're hardwired to say yes to most things, not knowing why we'd be justified in saying no to anything. The cost of all the cultural noise combined with the temptation of obligation causes us to miss God's calling—we live unfocused and frazzled.

There is one other thing in my office that snaps all the other stuff into perspective: a piece of artwork. Vanessa, one of my former assistants, gave the piece to Junanne and me on my birthday in 1999. It's two photos of sunsets set in one frame. One sunset is from Arkansas and the other from Alaska. The piece signified a new season, as our family was moving to Alaska from Arkansas. But it also captured the reality that life changes quickly and the sun will set on all of our lives.

Vanessa lived with grace and love as few do. A few years after we received this gift, Vanessa's sunset came unexpectedly. In just months after a cancer diagnosis, she died too soon, leaving behind a shocked church family and a grieving family.

Life is too short to live like an order of hash browns at a Waffle House. The time is now to focus your effort.

MEASURE WHAT MATTERS

Knowing what matters and measuring progress is how anything is built well. Whether it's a business, bridge, or a building; a team, a tower, or a massive vessel for shipping, measure what matters, or what you build will sink. This decision is one of the most consequential in the life you're building as you partner with God.

John Doerr authored the *New York Times* bestseller, *Measure What Matters.* There's not a successful business leader in America that hasn't read it or at least unknowingly worked the plan. Doerr's premise is simple and powerful: measure what matters for the success of your business. Focus on those metrics, and you'll have a good shot at success. Here's one of Doerr's more quotable statements from the book: "We must realize—and act on the realization—that if we try to focus on everything, we focus on nothing."[6]

IF YOU FOCUS ON WHAT MATTERS MOST, YOU'LL INVEST TIME AND ENERGY INTO AREAS THAT CAN MAKE YOU STRONG FOR THE LONG HAUL.

So here's what's obvious and predictable: if you focus on what matters most, you'll invest time and energy into areas that can make you strong for the long haul. This is true in every area of life and how you build your life.

How do we focus our effort in the direction of things that matter? Is God okay with us focusing our efforts on things we like to do? Where do we go to know God's will for our life?

These are great questions, God's not afraid of them, and He has answers.

Many people have never heard from God, but it's not because He is silent; it's because we just won't stop talking, moving, self-medicating, and people-pleasing (the biggest problem). We live lives that others want us to live or expect of us. Or we allow what others think to shape our focus even if they have no connection with God and are simply not wise counselors. We might even hate the direction we're going and feel like something is wrong, but we press on trying to live for the approval of someone other than God.

But God has something to say. And when God is aiming our life, there is no more extraordinary life to live. God's will for your life and what really matters is anchored in God's Word. There is nothing like joining God in His Word to discover direction for life and focus your efforts.

God's Will Is Written

Proverbs 29:18 is a verse used by many to underscore why we should catch God's vision for our life. The King James Version is often cited: "Where there is no vision, the people perish." It's a great verse, but rarely do you hear the rest of it. "But he that keepeth the law, happy is he."

Looking at it in the English Standard Version is more faithful to the original language, and it comes into great focus. "Where there is no prophetic vision the people cast off restraint [or, *the people are discouraged*], but blessed is he who keeps the law." You break down this verse, and it will launch you.

God wants you to have a clear vision for your life! God didn't save your life just to leave you aimless in life. He is passionate about your knowing who you are, where you're going, and that you're confident that you're tracking with His will for you. God's vision is written down! Tracking with the truth of God's Word is all the vision you need. God's Word becomes the guardrails for your life. His truth keeps you from getting in a ditch on one side or the other, and yet, out in front of you is blue sky.

God's vision encourages your soul! Any notion that God wants to steal your joy or diminish your life to do His will is inconsistent with the promises of God. John Piper puts a twist on the Westminster confession, and I believe it's spot on: "God is most glorified in us when we are most satisfied in him."[7] Enjoy God's vision; it's part of God's will.

God's Will Is Always Aimed at Our Growth

I had a man once ask me how to decide between two job offers. He wanted to know God's will. He was a man who loved God's Word, and he was actively taking down lies and raising the truth in his mind. What words I gave him, I'll give to you for almost any decision you're making.

I took him to 1 Thessalonians 4:3a: "For this is the will of God, your sanctification." Sanctification simply means to grow in faith, and we rely on God's grace and power. God wants you to make decisions based on your growth and spiritual trajectory. The most significant factor in decision-making needs to trump fiscal, geographical, familial, and professional considerations. All of those are important, but one rises above the rest: Will this decision serve to shrink you or grow you spiritually?

Knowing God's will isn't a game God plays. He's got a plan, and He wants you to follow it. You never have to settle for too little again. There's a higher calling than focusing your life on what is popular, accepted, politically correct, or even expected of you. When you measure your approval through the eyes of humans, something strange happens. You become deaf to the voice of God. But when you open God's Word, clear your mind, seek truth, and believe He wants to grow you, you can know God's will and go His way.

It's time for you to execute what matters most in life. Measuring what matters will enable you to build a life that honors God, enjoys Him, and takes hold of His promises. God has uniquely designed you. As you humbly surrender to God, He gives you fresh passion for things that matter and the gifts to pull it off. Agreeing with God to focus your effort around the passion and gifting He's planted in your soul is tremendous. Now let's go discover that.

YOUR GIFTS DISCOVER YOU

There is nothing quite like it. When you get a handle on your gifting and it converges with your passion—*boom*!—everything changes. Understanding spiritual gifts and how to discover them is more simple than we might imagine.

When Jesus ascended, He gave gifts to His people (Eph. 4:8). Spiritual gifts are the dynamo of the community of Christ followers. They have one purpose: "So with yourselves, since you are eager for manifestations of the Spirit, strive to excel in building up the church" (1 Cor. 14:12). When each person uses their spiritual gifts, people get better, stronger, and everybody wins. The best way to discover your spiritual gifts is to let your gifts find you.

In Bible college, I didn't know winning the student body president position would automatically sign me up to speak to all the students, professors, and faculty twice that year. I never aimed to be a speaker or evangelist. My goal was to get a degree and construct buildings around the globe for a dynamic mission organization. I was just there to hit the organization's minimum expectation of "one year of Bible college."

When I got up to speak at that first student government chapel, I was nervous and completely abandoned to God. Something happened that was supernatural: my spiritual gift found me. The place was pin-drop quiet as I poured out what God had put on my heart. The Holy Spirit was palpable in that room. I can honestly say it wasn't me; it was the Spirit that empowered me. After the chapel, the president of the college walked up to me and simply said, "You can't ignore your gifts of preaching and leadership. Lean into them, Karl."

I've seen it so many times since. Spiritual gifts find people when people get engaged in the lives of others. God loves to steer a moving "boat," even if it fearfully leaves the dock without knowing exactly where it's going. When you get moving, you'll find two things: 1. You begin to get pulled along with a gifting that lifts others. 2. Other people will, in time, recognize and affirm those gifts as your gifts are lifting the lives of those around you.

When your gifts discover you, it's a one-two punch: self-discovery and affirmation. God can and will direct you into your sweet spot when you move into the community of Christ followers and witness God indeed using your life to help others discover their gifts. And on this note of helping others, that's exactly how your gift is confirmed. Gifts are to edify. God gives them to build up the broader body of Christ. That's the ultimate test of hitting your unique design and role in the church.

Gifts "tests" are a great place to begin your search, but they're not the end-all. The very best way I've seen people discover gifts and receive affirmation is by engaging in the life and lives of the body of Christ. Explore and push the boundaries of conventional wisdom. Sometimes the gift you have is outside the box of what you might have imagined. The gifts God gives us can be completely different from any talents we use to do our job or enjoy a hobby.

If you try something and it's not a good fit, move to another slot and keep moving until you find a fit. Also, don't let people shift you or promote you out of your gifting. You can be crushing it in one area and slide into a role that is not your gift or your joy. Stay in the sweet spot with God. It's truly an adventure.

SWIFT WATER

Sometimes life teaches you lessons that you'll carry with you until you die. On a raft trip, God showed me why it's so essential to stay locked in with my passion and gifting. I think the lesson will stick with you as well.

The best staff bonding time I've ever had was on a river. The whole two days were quite remarkable. Loading about twenty church staff into rafts to float along twenty-six miles of the Little Susitna River was unique even by Alaskan standards. We caught fish, laughed at some of our rafts getting beached on sandbars, and even had a bear near our camp one night that caused someone to not make it all the way to the outhouse.

But day two turned into a race. I learned something right away about rafting on Alaskan rivers. You can row or paddle in your strength, but it leads to problems. On one side of the river, the currents slow to a trickle, and there's usually a sandbar to get stuck on. On the other side are trees and alder bushes overhanging the water and grabbing hold of clothing, hair, and arms; it's a mess, and you can get hurt.

The secret is this: find the swiftest part of the stream, and focus your effort on staying in the swift water. The swift slice of the river could carry you faster than all the effort exerted to win in your strength.

This directly applies to focused energy. When your energy is focused on getting into the swift water of your passion and gifting and staying there, you're going to be moving fast, and you're in for a ride. The swift water of your passion and gifting is going to be different than that of the others around you. You'll be tempted to try another part of the river. But always remember to focus your effort on what God has mapped out (Ps. 37:23). This doesn't mean that God won't call us into uncomfortable situations or ask us to accomplish tasks that are anything but fun . . . but even these things have deeper meaning when we're locked in on our passion and gifting.

ON MISSION!

If you tackle this resolution's application section, you'll have a statement you can carry with you wherever you go. A God-given personal mission statement doesn't need a budget, building, or position. Your passion and gifting are not constrained by person, place, or thing. Nothing and no one can stop what God has placed in you. When you land on your personal mission statement, you're ready to travel—anywhere!

In the introduction to this book I shared my personal mission statement. I'm so grateful I've been locked on this for over two decades. I'll mention it here again to help give you an idea how I came up with it. It is the most precise reflection of my passion and gifting. Here it is:

> I exist to inspire a spiritual revolution within the church that reaches the world.

This reflects some things about me that I discovered in short order after God transformed my life. It reflects my heart for the people of the world to hear the message of hope in Christ. It also reveals that I believe a revived church that is overthrowing religious pretense and is passionate about lost people is the best vehicle for the gospel. You can also get a glimpse of one other thing. I have gifts of preaching, leadership, and evangelism. Put these together, and God enables me to inspire people when I'm walking in the Spirit.

Everything I do is aimed at this. Even my roles of being a husband, father to adult children, and money manager are impacted by my gifting and passion. I don't change how God has designed me to fulfill my God-given roles. I express my gifting and passion through those roles.

But knowing my mission focuses me like nothing else can. I don't take a speaking gig that isn't linked to my personal mission statement. I now turn down offers to go into side hustles that are fun but off-mission for me. Being a pastor of a most amazingly diverse and passionate young church in Chicago fits my mission to a T. Being a morning radio host of a discipleship-oriented show that reaches over 250,000 people a week across Chicagoland and leverages my inspirational gifts is in my wheelhouse. And this very book is entirely aimed at my personal mission statement, like an arrow at the bull's-eye.

You can do this! Let me help!

APPLICATION:
How to Focus Effort

IDENTIFY YOUR PASSIONS – It's time to look deep within. Think below the surface and pray for clarity. I find that being quiet and focused produces the most accurate results. Discovering what God has placed within you is like looking for treasure. Remove from your thinking all the perceived constraints like finances, distance, and your capacity; anything that may limit your thinking has to go. These questions will help you narrow in on your passions as you search your heart.

- What issue gets your heart beating fast?
- What people do you most want to help?
- What big problem do you want to solve?
- What is the solution you want to provide?

IDENTIFY YOUR GIFTS – Letting God's gifts discover *you* requires that you look outside of yourself and hear from others. Honest input of others is most critical. Receiving feedback from several different people who know you and have seen you engage with others is essential. Stress for them how important it is that they not feel like you need to be *affirmed* as much as you desire your true gifts to be *confirmed*. These questions will help you determine your gifts as you hear what others see, not just what you believe.

- Have you seen me lift up people?
- How specifically was I used to lift up people?
- What do I offer people that would be lacking without me?
- What would you like to see me focus on to strengthen my gifting?

WRITE YOUR PERSONAL MISSION STATEMENT – Few people will write a personal mission statement, but the few who do will make a big difference in the world and have greater joy. This is not a one-shot exercise. The best statements will be honed over time. But your first draft will be reasonably close if you've followed the steps above to identify your passions and gifts.

- Place all the keywords from your passion and gifts exercise on a paper.
- Construct a statement that incorporates the keywords and any other descriptors. It's no problem if it's a run-on sentence or a small paragraph.
- Crunch the statement down into something punchy and memorable.
- Ask someone who loves you and who you trust if the statement is true to who you are.
- Place your personal mission statement in prominent places to remind you.
- Keep refining and owning your personal mission statement.
- LIVE your personal mission statement!

Chapter 10

RESOLUTION #7
REDEEM TIME

Time is what we want most, but what, alas! we use worst.[1]

William Penn

I took the challenge! Hugh Salisbury, professor of pastoral studies, asked for volunteers to track a week of their life. The goal was to account for every half hour for a whole week and measure how well we were redeeming the time. This sounded right up my alley. My dad was one of the most efficient men I knew, and he had trained me well. This challenge would reveal that I knew how to bust my tail with the best.

With a full college load, new bride, construction jobs on the side, position as a part-time youth pastor, and a son on the way, I was swamped. There was zero discretionary time . . . of that I was sure. I was looking forward to putting my charted week up against anyone else.

Professor Salisbury took a particular interest in me and a few others.

He was bold and dared to ask questions few men could get out of their mouths. He was honest about sexual temptation, compromise, and how to order your private life in a way that cut Satan off at the pass. He had a heart for pastoral students to be men who heard from God one day, "Well done, my good and faithful servant."

Central to his discipleship of me and a handful of others was helping us understand how we handled the time God gave us. He believed a man who could account for his time was poised for a "fruitful and shameless life." In his seventies, this extremely fit, white-haired man would roar with passion about being more focused on who we were, not what we knew. In retrospect, Professor Salisbury was preparing each of us for being a pastor *and* a good man; he never just assumed the two went together.

The challenge began. I found that the first two days caused me to be quite aware of my time and slightly more disciplined than I might otherwise have been. On day three, I got a bit nervous. I had a ton to get done, and the awareness raised by tracking time caused me to jump on assignments and tasks more quickly. Now I was wrapping things up, knocking papers out, and prepping for messages and classroom presentations like never before. I was even taking Junanne on dates, having deep talks at our favorite yogurt shop.

By day four, five, and six, I started fudging my tracking. Something that took fifteen minutes, I rounded up to thirty minutes. I even panicked a bit because the first three days had been so productive I was struggling to find things to do. I thought, "What is happening?" I told Junanne I was feeling like a bit of a slacker. Her words made me feel a bit better: "Bub, you're the most productive guy I know." I may have been productive relative to some, but the lesson Prof Salisbury wanted me to learn was getting driven home. Day seven I just wrote off to a day of rest. I figured I couldn't get penalized for being a Biblicist.

At our next class, the professor asked who wanted to share what they'd learned. Every guy had the same experience; it was a race to apologize for not spending time more wisely. The banter was loud and spirited. Hugh Salisbury just stood back and listened. Then he spoke. "Gentlemen, I didn't ask you to take this challenge to shame you. I desire that you understand just how much time God has graciously given you. And that by understanding, you will learn to redeem time. Come on, men, it's right there in the Bible!" That class with Professor Salisbury challenged and encouraged me; the one-week challenge changed my life.

TRACKING THE NUMBERS

This resolution aims not to get you worshiping work or becoming consumed with minutes of the day; it's to help you redeem the time as a way of honoring God. It's to work hard, play hard, and learn to recharge without the shame of a wasted life.

Squandered time is more than lost time; it's the loss of a precious commodity to help us live in certain victory and wisdom, as we'll see clearly in God's Word. This may be hard to hear, but it's the truth—wasted time diminishes the potential impact that comes from your life. And if you don't redeem time, you're letting too much joy slip by. But the flip side is equally valid. If you want to thrive and leave a mark in this life, redeem time.

As I shared in the resolution Kill Sin, getting the time spent on our smartphones and tablets under control can curb sin in remarkable ways. The machines will make us or break us. Below are two statistics that are shocking and alarming. They should reinforce for you the war we are in for our time.

- The average time US adults (18+) spent with electronic media (non-work related) per day is over 10 hours.[2]
- "Americans averaged more than 5 hours of free time per day; no subgroup reported having less than 4.5 hours of free time."[3]

The metadata in these studies is informative and convicting. But the empirical evidence of our media exposure and "free time" is simply mind-boggling.

HAPPY ANNIVERSARY?

Early on in our marriage, Junanne was seeing precious time slip away; I just didn't see it as clearly. I wasn't hooked on sitcoms or movies but I loved watching news from multiple angles, and there weren't too many sports I didn't enjoy watching.

We had been married for about a decade. Our two little kids were precious to us, and we knew the value of investing in their lives. Getting time together was more complicated, and we wondered how we'd make the time for everything. Something had to give.

Our anniversary was coming in a week, and I thought I'd offer Junanne the ultimate gift. I went to her and said, "Babe, why don't you think about what you'd love for our anniversary." She said she'd think about it. Two days later, she said she knew what she wanted. I was excited. Then she lowered the boom. "I'd like a gift of us turning off the television for the next year." I was stunned and asked her with a chuckle, "Got any other ideas?"

Well, I gave it to her. The first two weeks were tough. I didn't know how much of a challenge this crazy gift would be. But in time, we got used to it. We had a ton of extra time, and I turned watching select games into a father-son experience for our son. I'd plan times when my son and I would head to a sports bar that was fit for a young boy. We'd get the nachos, and turn it into a real bonding experience. Because they were less frequent than just plopping down in front of the TV, they became memorable. Our son remembers these as special times with dad to talk about life.

After the year was over, our appetite for television had been reeled in significantly. We found ourselves not wanting to go back to it as often as had been the habit. I've never regretted that year, and I look back at it as a paradigm and behavior-shifting season that's paying dividends to this day.

GET OUT OF THE MUSHY MIDDLE

Our approach to time is all wrong. We enter a day and find ourselves getting beat by the clock. Either we don't work hard and aren't as productive as we'd like, or we don't seem to find the time to relax and truly wind down. Redeeming time is not about being busy. You can take a nap to the glory of God. You can sit and cuddle with your kid and honor God big-time. The goal is to take the initiative on time so we can live redemptive, shame-free lives.

The first time I stepped onto a tennis court, the coach said I was standing where most people think you stand. He called where I stood No Man's Land. He explained that playing tennis requires we play back for the volley or move to the net. He displayed how you can't get a racquet on a ball in No Man's Land, let alone win a point. This is often how we live with the clock. We don't play at the net or back for the volley. We're on the court, but time is passing us by.

I like to call this living in the mushy middle. The mushy middle is where Israel spent forty years. As you'll see in a moment, Moses learned a valuable lesson by forty years of wandering in the desert. A generation of God's kids would never taste the fruit of the promised land because they lacked the faith and wisdom to move onto the promise despite the giants.

The mushy middle is how Laodicea lived (Rev. 3:14–22)—neither hot nor cold, just lukewarm. Many wrongly believe that Jesus was calling the church to get red hot in their commitment to Him, but that's not the case. Jesus was appealing to the church, dripping with modern prosperity, to get out of the mushy middle. No one likes mushy anything and certainly not the mushy middle.

SELF-HELP VS. GOD'S HELP

When we think of time redemption, we instantly think of productivity. That's undoubtedly a by-product. Most self-help authors focus on the productivity angle alone. But the real promise is so much more. The promise of redeeming time is immense. Moses saw a direct link between tracking time and gaining a heart of wisdom. How insightful that a man who wasn't even going to cross the river into the promised land, prayed this: "So teach us to number our days that we may get a heart of wisdom" (Ps. 90:12). Let's break down this song that Moses wrote:

- Teach us – Moses appealed to God for a specific thing that would benefit the people.
- To number our days – The brevity of life with all its challenges and opportunities stood out in the mind of Moses,

who had been shepherding God's people. Moses was resolved about the need to track time and redeem it all to God's glory.

- That we may get a heart of wisdom – Surprise! Redeeming time is inextricably linked to wisdom. What a striking correlation. Redeeming time is not just a wise move; it's how we *gain* wisdom.

To do this right, we need one thing, according to Charles Spurgeon: "Numeration is a child's exercise in arithmetic, but in order to number their days aright the best of men **need the Lord's teaching**. We are more anxious to count the stars than our days, and yet the latter is by far more practical."[4]

REDEEMING TIME IS NOT JUST A WISE MOVE; IT'S HOW WE *GAIN* WISDOM.

Psalm 90 isn't a biblical anomaly. Scripture links time management almost exclusively to wisdom: "Look carefully then how you walk, not as unwise but as wise, making the best use of the time, because the days are evil" (Eph. 5:15–16). This anchor thought from the apostle Paul deserves the same kind of breakdown.

- Look carefully then how you walk – Paul wrote to the church in Ephesus that a self-examined life is an overcoming life. We can't head off willy-nilly into our days, or we'll walk into the mushy middle.

- Not as unwise but as wise – Wisdom here is directly linked to time redemption. Wisdom and accounting for time walk hand in hand.

- Making the best use of time – The "best use" of time implies intentionality. We can't let hours pass without measuring where they're going and how they're spent.

- Because the days are evil – The enemy of time redemption is not just our flesh; we walk in a world with bad intentions. Evil tries to push us into foolish choices, pull us away from life-giving relationships, and suck us into moral compromises that leave us empty. The battle for time redemption must be fought on our knees because evil never sleeps.

So let's put a myth to death right now. Time management isn't a self-help thing; it's a God-help thing. Time does not come to us redeemed. Every minute we receive is a gift from God. To redeem time means to "buy back" or "gain possession." We can do it as we like. We will either redeem time or squander time; there is no grey zone. I want you to know how simple, yet powerful, this can be. Simply stop and surrender your calendar to God. God will leverage all the resolutions up to this point to help you focus on what matters most. Yes, God helps us manage our lives by the days and hours.

TIME MANAGEMENT ISN'T A SELF-HELP THING; IT'S A GOD-HELP THING. TIME DOES NOT COME TO US REDEEMED.

Spiritual vitality and living with excellence are no mystery. Here's the secret that wise people get: a few minutes of planning and managing the minutes of our day creates clarity, keeps us on track with God's vision for our lives, and keeps us out of the weeds of regret.

So get after it. Resolve to find a system that accounts for your days/hours/minutes—it's God's idea. Plan your time before someone else's plan captures your time. Time management isn't selfishness; it's stewardship. Don't let "evil" snatch another day from your life. Today is loaded with potential. Get every bit of it with God's help!

THE TALE OF TWO BEDTIMES

Why talk about bedtime when we're talking about redeeming time? Because a wise way to redeem time is to have energy in the morning that carries through the day. The Scriptures are clear about sleep: "It is in vain that you rise up early and go late to rest, eating the bread of anxious toil; for he gives to his beloved sleep" (Ps. 127:2). Simply put: burning the candle at both ends is not God's plan.

Sleep is undervalued by many. The Sleep Foundation has studied the benefits of sleep and learned this.

> Sleep is just as critical to our body as other basic functions of survival like eating, drinking, and breathing. Sleep is needed for a number of reasons, including energy conservation, restoration of our tissues and cognitive function, emotion regulation, and immune health.[5]

Sleep matters, big time! Just one unredeemed hour can impact the next twenty-three. It's undeniably true that the sleep we get tonight will impact our day tomorrow. The Sleep Foundation offers solid research that should wake us up:

> For most adults, at least seven hours of sleep each night is needed for proper cognitive and behavioral functions. An insufficient amount of sleep can lead to serious repercussions. Some studies have shown sleep deprivation leaves people

vulnerable to attention lapses, reduced cognition, delayed reactions, and mood shifts.[6]

Be careful. Studies reveal that people can believe they're doing great, when actually they've just adjusted to a way of living that is off its "A" game and possibly headed for trouble.

People can develop a sort of tolerance to chronic sleep deprivation. Even though their brains and bodies struggle due to lack of sleep, they may not be aware of their own deficiencies because less sleep feels normal to them. Additionally, lack of sleep has been linked to a higher risk for certain diseases and medical conditions. These include obesity, type 2 diabetes, high blood pressure, heart disease, stroke, poor mental health, and early death.[7]

Sleep is also the time when your body is working to assimilate vitamins and minerals, getting rid of toxins, and balancing hormones. Sleep is just plain good for you! Getting enough sleep can be challenging, to say the least. I don't know anyone who hasn't battled sleep schedules. I don't know what your story is, but I'll share my two "tales" of bedtime. See if either of these stories sound familiar . . .

Tale #1

I've battled getting to bed over the years. Feeling like I want to "wind down" from a long day, I can easily slide into a gripping podcast, binge-watch news, chase the rabbit down the hole of a Twitter thread, and stream documentaries on ships colliding with docks. I've even watched a rerun of *Gilligan's Island* on occasion. Then comes the walk of shame, which you've probably taken yourself. On top of heading off to bed late, you're kicking yourself. The clock can't be turned back.

The problem isn't one hour wasted; the domino effect is in motion. The next morning, the alarm goes off, and you're off. But you're not on your game. The whole day is a bit of a struggle. Things that aren't that big a deal bother you deeply. You feel cranky and would love a nap. Relationships are strained, and even if you can hide it, you're just not loving life. The crazy part is that we often repeat this routine.

Tale #2

Over a decade ago, I resolved to honor God by going to bed early enough to get the seven to eight hours of sleep I needed to be my best the next day. The reason for this is biblical and practical. The surest way to honor God was to fight off all temptations to stay up.

I fought, and still fight, for better sleep, and it is worth the battle. My energy increases throughout the day, and I have found that I have also increased my capacity to fulfill my calling. Sleep goes a long way to helping me listen to God and to be aware of how I speak to people. Focus on projects, creativity, and engagement in meetings has been a bit of the fruit of hitting the hay early.

Sleep has been a necessity for me as I rise at about 3 a.m. to do a radio show on weekdays from 5 to 9 a.m. In the last four years, I've also held down a lead pastor position at a church we planted called 180 Chicago. God has been gracious. I have time and energy to love my wife well and connect deeply with those friends who call me forward.

Below are some of the strategic moves that made all the difference in my life, and I'm confident they will in yours.

- Get on a sleep schedule. Training your body to go to bed at a set time is powerful.

- Lower the temperature in your room. We sleep more soundly in cooler temperatures.
- Exercise your body regularly. At a minimum, walk and get deep breaths of fresh air.
- Finish eating about two hours before you sleep. A full stomach competes with rest.
- Turn off your screens an hour before bed. Blue light suppresses melatonin production.

I used to pride myself on how much sleep I could "get by on." This is crazy talk. One of the very best ways to redeem time is to get sleep. Fight for sleep. Kill the sleep robbers in your life. Sleep is one of the best blocks of time we can invest into our life. You honor God by getting enough sleep because the next day your time has a better shot at being redeemed.

SAY NO TO TIME STEALERS, SAY YES TO GOD

When you get up in the morning, you have a big choice to make: Who or what will control your time? If you don't allow God to take control of your time, it will fall to the control of other forces, and the results are never good.

In his book *Ordering Your Private World*, Gordon MacDonald lists four laws of unmanaged time:[8]

- Unmanaged time flows toward my weaknesses.
- Unmanaged time comes under the influence of dominant people in my world.

- Unmanaged time surrenders to the demands of all emergencies.
- Unmanaged time gets invested in things that gain public acclamation.

To keep us away from our calling, passion, and God's promises, I believe Satan must lick his chops when we release control of our time to anything other than God. Our natural weaknesses, dominant people, emergency demands, and public acclaim are all drivers that will take over the hours of our day if we let them.

Saying no to the wrong things (which can also be *good* things) can feel impossible. But there is a secret to successfully redeeming time that removes the pain of saying no: say yes to God! Numbering our days and redeeming time is best done proactively. Like staking a mining claim in the gold rush, you need to look at your days as a treasure and stake claim to your days, so someone doesn't jump your claim. It happens.

Knowing where to focus your effort is liberating. It allows you to find the right places to work, serve, and invest your time. Determining the roles you have in your life is the primary way to begin ordering your life and redeeming the time. Let me show you how this works for me.

When you have a personal mission statement, it will guide your life into key roles. Getting yourself out of jobs and commitments not aligned with your unique design could take time but keep you moving toward your calling. As you focus your effort in aligning your life with your personal mission statement, you'll find areas of responsibility emerging. Some of your roles may be the result of being married and having children.

Identifying the key roles in your life becomes the bigger YES for scheduling your time. Let me share with you my primary roles just as I have them written in my daily journal. Some of yours will be the same but many will be different.

- Husband/Father - Love Junanne as Christ loved the church and pour wisdom into my kids.
- Leader/Pastor - Coach and develop a dynamic team that leads a prevailing church.
- Motivator/Evangelist - Deliver transformational content in the Holy Spirit's power.
- Financial Steward - Reduce expenses and increase income so we can give generously.
- Temple Manager - Give my body the rest, nutrients, and exercise needed to fulfill my calling.

Notice I'm not listing the jobs I do; we need to see beyond our jobs and embrace our calling. God has us in positions for something greater than punching a clock or filling a slot. When you align your time around those things God is calling you to be, you'll find more joy and fulfillment from a single day than you previously could muster in a week.

Redeeming time redeems life. It brings order to disorder. Time with children is more intentional. Time at work has fresh meaning. Time for strengthening your body has a greater purpose. Time with your spouse or friends is set aside for quality. Redeeming time moves you from being reactive to proactive. Agree with God to redeem time, and He gets the glory, and you get the joy.

LIFE BY THE LIST VS. LIFE FROM THE CENTER

One of the biggest mistakes we make in redeeming time is looking at our life as a list. We put the most valuable things at the top. As we go down the list, we put some stuff as lesser in importance—we force ourselves to rank the value of what we do. But that's just not how God wants us to live. Paul spoke of eating and drinking as being opportunities to glorify God. "So, whether you eat or drink, or whatever you do, do all to the glory of God" (1 Cor. 10:31). He also had a more general call on our life to see everything we do as a way to say thank You, God. "And whatever you do, in word or deed, do everything in the name of the Lord Jesus, giving thanks to God the Father through him" (Col. 3:17).

What follows are two ways to look at your life and roles. The first is more conventional and reflects how people prioritize their roles, elevating some and diminishing others. Most Christians always put God at the top. For the sake of reinforcing Resolution 2, I'll call it "Join God." I call this "life by the list."

LIFE BY THE LIST

1. Join God
2. Husband/Father
3. Leader/Pastor
4. Motivator/Evangelist
5. Financial Steward
6. Temple Manager

This is how we get into trouble: how these roles are "ranked" is subjective, and we run the risk of valuing some higher than others. Some people might put "financial steward" closer to the top because of the impact of finances on every part of life. Some may not even have "temple manager" on the list, while others might list roles that would never make your list. With Life by the List you may rank some of these roles higher than I did, but whatever lands nearer to the bottom will get the scraps of our attention and focused effort.

Everyone's list will be a bit different. Others may see some roles as not even "making the list"! For instance, Junanne is a good artist. The work is not only refreshing for her; it fulfills a sense of calling. Some people might think artist isn't worth listing. But the God of all creation delights in Junanne doing her artwork. She finds the pleasure of God in painting, and others see God's hand through her work.

Whatever roles God has called you to fill, there is nothing of lesser importance than another. The problem of ranking roles in our mind, thereby diminishing some, is that we may not commit time to what we, or others, consider "lesser" roles; or if we do, we may end up feeling judged or guilty. This is tragic and easily solved by looking at your life and roles in a more biblically sound way.

LIFE FROM THE CENTER

Notice something remarkable with this perspective. We see joining God as central to everything. And all that we do is giving glory to

God. There is no visual ranking of value, so we are more emotionally, mentally, and spiritually free to let the power of God flow into every role we fill. While we will be more focused on one role over another on certain days or during more intense seasons of focus, no role is lesser than the other. This allows us to now look at what's most important, and that's tapping into God's power as we join Him in spiritual disciplines. Redeeming time now has the biblical structure and foundation needed to apply this with robust confidence.

APPLICATION:
How to Redeem Time

IDENTIFY YOUR KEY ROLES – This can be done in a couple of hours. Think in terms of where God is calling you to focus your effort. Even if there are commitments in your life that are not in your sweet spot, give them a place in your various roles. God can redeem anything if it's surrendered to Him. This exercise may reveal that you have too many irons in the fire or that you've diminished or neglected what God has called you to be. Great! That can be worked out in time. The main thing is to determine your top three to six roles and get them down on paper.

GET A GOOD DAY PLANNER – There are too many distractions in our generation to try and wing it or remember what is most valuable. The way to say no to lesser things is to say yes to God. Taking control of the hours in your day allows you to have legitimate appointments that other lesser things can't infringe upon. Many are finding that although there are some slick apps to help redeem time, it's better to see it on paper. Taking the time to look at a bigger picture and filling in what's vital will help you own your hours. (Consider trying the planner I designed for my own use. You'll find more information on the resource page or by going to 7Resolutions.com.)

BLOCK TIME THE DAY BEFORE – When you block out time, you're not saying things can't move and shift, but you're staking claim to what's valuable. This is an art form, and I have produced resources that will help you know how to time block. In short, time blocking requires that you look at the highest value activities or appointments in each role you fill. Determining the most important things and putting them in place makes it more likely they will get done.

ASSESS, ADJUST, AND CELEBRATE – The pressure is off. You won't master this overnight. I've been using a planner for forty years, and I still fail to follow through at times. But I can see the correlation between redeeming time and my joy and fulfillment. This is a tool God will use more than you. He will reveal things you need to see. It won't all be beautiful, but it will be beneficial. Know this: God is cheering for you as you redeem time and grow in wisdom.

Conclusion

TRACTION AND MOTIVATION

◊

You are among a select group who made it to the end. Something has stirred you to believe that God has more, and you desire to experience it. I've got some good news: this is not the end; it's just the beginning. Believe it!

But I've saved an aspect for the urgency of this book until now. I'm not a prophet, in the sense of predicting the future, but I do believe that religious liberties will continue to erode in America and abroad. This will cause Christ followers to be tested in unique ways.

The need for the church to make disciples who are rejecting passivity is now. The time has come to grow up in Christ and come alive! This is the hour to prepare for spiritual battles that will test us and reveal what we're made of. My challenge is for you to seize the day, and join a growing number of God's kids who want to survive, thrive, and shine radiantly no matter what may come.

So, I invite you to make this book more than something you read.

I want you to agree with God to do something bold: to make the 7 Resolutions part of who you are and join a larger community who are with you in passion, spirit, and practice. In every race that is run there are two things every person needs: good traction and the right motivation. My aim is providing you these in practical ways.

Cross country ski racing wasn't my strength. I didn't have the natural distance capacity to climb hills, descend slopes, and cover many kilometers through forests all while kicking and poling away. But two factors made all the difference, and I could compete well when these two came together.

Waxing the Skis

We had a wax shed in Alaska that proved invaluable. Snow conditions changed daily, and so did the need to apply the right wax to match the snow's temperature and moisture content. Without the right wax, you'd either be stuck to the snow with no gliding ability, or your skis would be so slick you'd be spinning out and going nowhere. Getting the right sticky stuff for the conditions gave you the perfect amount of traction.

Training with Peers

Having a few other skiers to train, struggle alongside, and celebrate with helped keep us motivated when lung capacity was waning. We would shout encouragement to each other and take turns in the lead to help break the wind. Being surrounded by peers would keep you moving when you might have quit if you were alone. Training with peers gives you the motivation needed to compete in a way that positions you to win.

I've taken steps to provide the traction and motivation for you to succeed in the 7 Resolutions. It's not a one-and-done when it comes to the resolutions. To grow proficient in joining God, thinking truth, killing sin, choosing friends, taking risks, focusing effort, and redeeming time, we grow as we flex the muscle of dependence on God and remain diligent in moving with Him.

You desire to compete well and get some small wins under your belt that produce an increasing number of victories in your life. Success is not measured by having no setbacks and not getting stuck. This side of heaven we will battle daily, but it's worth the fight. Leaning into the 7 Resolutions may intensify spiritual wars, but the breakthroughs will truly gratify your heart. My commitment is to provide traction and motivation to help you through these battles and bring you out the other side amazed at God's grace.

God is calling you to stand, see, and walk in His strength. He wants to give you a vision of adventure and fresh victories for His glory and your joy. He invites you to dream again, daring to take Him at His word. Never again apologize for wanting a win. Your desire for victory over what holds you back is placed there by God. There will be battles, sacrifices, scars, fire-forged friendships, setbacks, risk-taking, little conquests, and celebrations. It's worth it all. Let's run this race together.

RESOURCES

My deepest desire is for you to experience God's power, conquer your biggest battles, and thrive as a disciple of Christ. As you begin the 7 Resolutions, my team and I want to come alongside you and equip you with practical resources to help you win. Most of these are free, and new resources will be added. The following resources are available here: 7Resolutions.com

- ◊ **7 Resolutions Assessment** – This will reveal your areas of strength and the areas that would benefit from focused attention. We will provide you with a simple strategy to move forward in those specific resolutions—a strategy that can be shared with the friends you've chosen to journey with you into the 7 Resolutions.
- ◊ **Day Planner** – This original planner integrates the 7 Resolutions, your unique roles, a yearly overview, a four-month overview, and a daily view. Each planner covers four months, making for a manageable size and three fresh starts per year.
- ◊ **Videos** – These short videos will further expand on important concepts in the book. There will be an introductory video for each chapter. Testimonial videos will be a source of encouragement from others who are taking hold of God's promises.

- ◊ **Blogs** – Karl and other guest authors will supplement the content of the book with both theological and practical posts to know and apply the truths that will continue to set you free.
- ◊ **Study Guide** – This practical guide is perfect to use with small groups or a few friends, or to just take a deeper dive on your own.

I'm praying that God gives you great strength and courage for the path ahead. My greatest joy is hearing stories of life-change, so be sure to send us your story by visiting 7Resolutions.com.

Blessings,
Karl

ACKNOWLEDGMENTS

The kind of people you have around you can take you places you could never go alone—this book is a testament to that.

Randall Payleitner, associate publisher of Moody Publishers, promised I'd love his team, and he was spot-on. Amy Simpson sharpened my big concept ideas. Amanda Cleary brought a sharp eye for detailed editing. Derek Thornton and Erik Peterson broke us out of the box for design elements. Jeremy Slager brought together a team to get this work seen. Janice Todd leveraged her expertise to publicity. Connor Sterchi and his proofreaders appear to have fine-tooth combs. To the rest who played a role at Moody Publishers, I'm genuinely grateful. It's been a joy.

Those in my inner circle are invaluable. Ajit Christopher did a terrific job at research and proofing the central passages and citations. Katie Christopher offered great insights with nuanced ideas that added flavor and clarity. My son and daughter have been two of my best cheerleaders, and my wife is a constant source of hope and encouragement.

To my morning team and the listeners of *Karl and Crew Mornings* and the members of 180 Chicago Church, I can only say thank you from the bottom of my heart. Your love for God and passion for following

Him have only served to catalyze my firm belief in God's power to take hold of His promises.

My biggest thanks are reserved for the God above all gods, my faithful friend, and the fuel for my soul—Father, Son, and the Holy Spirit.

NOTES

Introduction—Radical Change Is Possible

1. "God Helps Those Who Help Themselves," Wikipedia, https://en.wikipedia.org/wiki/God_helps_those_who_help_themselves.
2. "Survey: Salvation through Christ Attracts Just One in Three Adults; More Believe It Can Be Earned," Cultural Research Center, August 4, 2020, https://www.arizonachristian.edu/wp-content/uploads/2020/08/AWVI-2020-Release-08-Perceptions-of-Sin-and-Salvation.pdf.
3. Merriam-Webster, "Self-Help," https://www.merriam-webster.com/dictionary/self-help.

Chapter 1 – Wrecked

1. John Wooden and Steve Jamison, *Wooden on Leadership* (New York: McGraw-Hill eBooks, 2009), 202.
2. "New Years Resolution Statistics," Statistic Brain Research Institute, 2018, https://www.statisticbrain.com/new-years-resolution-statistics/.

Chapter 2 – Recovery

1. Rick Warren, *The Purpose Driven Life: What on Earth Am I Here For?* (Grand Rapids: Zondervan, ePub Edition, 2018), 31.
2. Dietrich Bonhoeffer, *The Cost of Discipleship* (London: SCM Press, 2015), 61.
3. Richard Feloni, "Tim Ferriss Lives His Life According to an Ancient Greek Quote that Helps Him Prepare for the Worst," *Business Insider*, December 1, 2017, https://www.businessinsider.com/tim-ferriss-favorite-quote-greek-philosopher-archilochus-2017-12.
4. Dallas Willard, "General Introduction to NavPress Spiritual Formation Line," June 1, 1997, https://conversatio.org/media-room/general-introduction-to-navpress-spiritual-formation-line/.
5. Andrew Murray, *Humility: The Path to Holiness* (Morgantown, KY: Tole Publishing, 2018), 10, Kindle.

6. C. S. Lewis, *The Weight of Glory: And Other Addresses* (New York: HarperCollins, 2009), 20, eBook.

Chapter 3 – The 7 Resolutions

1. *The Works of Jonathan Edwards* (Orange, CT: Samizdat Express, 1834), 142.
2. Andrew Murray, *Humility: The Path to Holiness* (Morgantown, KY: Tole Publishing, 2018), 10, Kindle.

Chapter 4 – Resolution #1: Join God

1. D. L. Moody, "*From Onward*, quoted in S.S. Times," *Peloubet's Select Notes on the International Lessons* (Holliston, MA: W. A. Wilde Co., 1918), 88.
2. Merriam-Webster, "Supernatural," https://www.merriam-webster.com/dictionary/supernatural.
3. Wyatt North, *The Life and Writings of Saint Augustine* (Wyatt North Publishing, 2021), 391.
4. Dallas Willard, *The Great Omission: Reclaiming Jesus's Essential Teachings on Discipleship* (New York: HarperCollins, 2006), 78, eBook.

Chapter 5 – Resolution #2: Think Truth

1. Dallas Willard, *Hearing God: Developing a Conversational Relationship with God* (Downers Grove, IL: InterVarsity Press, 2012), 12.
2. Eric Pooley, "Grins, Gore, and Videotape: The Trouble with Local TV News," *New York*, October 9, 1989, vol. 22, no. 40, 37.
3. Austin Perlmutter, "How Negative News Distorts Our Thinking," *Psychology Today*, September 19, 2019, https://www.psychologytoday.com/us/blog/the-modern-brain/201909/how-negative-news-distorts-our-thinking.
4. Gigen Mammoser, "The FOMO Is Real: How Social Media Increases Depression and Loneliness," Healthline, December 9, 2018, https://www.healthline.com/health-news/social-media-use-increases-depression-and-loneliness.
5. Elizabeth Hall, "Why Family Hurt Is So Painful," *Psychology Today*, March 27, 2017, https://www.psychologytoday.com/us/blog/conscious-communication/201703/why-family-hurt-is-so-painful.
6. Caroline Leaf, *Switch on Your Brain: The Key to Peak Happiness, Thinking, and Health* (Grand Rapids: Baker Books, 2013), 78.
7. John Lynch, Bruce McNicol, and Bill Thrall, *The Cure: What If God Isn't Who You Think He Is and Neither Are You* (Phoenix, AZ: Trueface, 2011), 33.

Chapter 6 – Resolution #3: Kill Sin

1. John Owen, *The Mortification of Sin* (Edinburgh: Banner of Truth, 2004), 113, Kindle.

2. "Pornography Survey Statistics," Proven Men, 2014, https://www.provenmen.org/pornography-survey-statistics-2014.
3. "Competing Worldviews Influence Today's Christians," Barna Group, May 9, 2017, https://www.barna.com/research/competing-worldviews-influence-todays-christians.
4. Christian Podcast Central, "WWUTT: Sin Means to Miss the Mark?," November 25, 2016, https://christianpodcastcentral.com/wwutt-sin-means-to-miss-the-mark/.
5. Dictionary.com, "kill shot," https://www.dictionary.com/browse/kill-shot.
6. John Piper, "Kill Sin by the Spirit," Desiring God, February 17, 2002, http://www.desiringgod.org/messages/kill-sin-by-the-spirit.
7. Joseph Price et al., "How Much More XXX Is Generation X Consuming? Evidence of Changing Attitudes and Behaviors Related to Pornography Since 1973," *Journal of Sex Research* 53, no. 1 (January 2016): 19, https://doi.org/10.1080/00224499.2014.1003773.
8. "Internet Pornography by the Numbers: A Significant Threat to Society," Webroot, https://www.webroot.com/us/en/resources/tips-articles/internet-pornography-by-the-numbers.
9. Asheritah Ciuciu, *Full: Food, Jesus, and the Battle for Satisfaction* (Chicago: Moody, 2017), 18.
10. Ibid., 45.

Chapter 7 – Resolution #4: Choose Friends

1. C. S. Lewis, *Selected Literary Essays: A Study in Medieval Tradition* (New York: Harper Collins, 2013), 158, eBook.
2. Content in this section was previously published at: https://www.moodyradio.org/programs/karl-and-crew-mornings/2020/09/9-29/?
3. "Partners in Crime: When Do Friends Conspire to Eat More Chocolate?" University of Chicago, May 21, 2014, https://phys.org/news/2014-05-partners-crime-friends-conspire-chocolate.html.
4. Catherine T. Shea, "Low on Self-Control? Surrounding Yourself with Strong-Willed Friends May Help," Association for Psychological Science, April 9, 2013, https://www.psychologicalscience.org/news/releases/low-on-self-control-surrounding-yourself-with-strong-willed-friends-may-help.html.
5. *Merriam-Webster*, s.v. "game changer," last updated September 12, 2021, https://www.merriam-webster.com/dictionary/game%20changer.
6. Jim Stovall, "Horse Sense," TimMaurer.com, January 16, 2012, https://timmaurer.com/2012/01/16/horse-sense.
7. J. D. Greear, "Friendship: You Were Made for It . . . and It Makes You," J. D. Greear Ministries, June 4, 2015, https://jdgreear.com/friendship-you-were-made-for-it-and-it-makes-you.

8. Timothy Keller with Kathy Keller, *The Meaning of Marriage: Facing the Complexities of Commitment with the Wisdom of God* (New York: Penguin, 2011), 112.

Chapter 8 – Resolution #5: Take Risks

1. John Piper, *Risk Is Right: Better to Lose Your Life Than to Waste It* (Wheaton, IL: Crossway, 2013).
2. Content in this section was previously published at the author's blog: http://www.karlclauson.com/blog/tag/vision?
3. Quoted in "The Missionary Herald" in *The Baptist Magazine* Vol. 35 (January 1843), 41.
4. Henry and Melvin Blackaby, *Experiencing the Spirit: The Power of Pentecost Every Day* (Colorado Springs, CO: Multnomah Books, 2009), 7.
5. William L. Holladay, *A Concise Hebrew and Aramaic Lexicon of the Old Testament: Based upon the Lexical Work of Ludwig Koehler and Walter Baumgartner* (Leiden: Brill, 2000), 315–16.

Chapter 9 – Resolution #6: Focus Effort

1. Bill Walsh, Steve Jamison, and Craig Walsh, *The Score Takes Care of Itself: My Philosophy of Leadership* (New York: Penguin Publishing Group, 2009), Kindle.
2. Ibid., 20.
3. Lydia Dishman, "Turning Information Overload Into Knowledge," *Fast Company*, May 10, 2012, https://www.fastcompany.com/1836838/turning-information-overload-knowledge.
4. Canela López, "7 Tech Executives Who Raise Their Kids Tech-Free or Seriously Limit Their Screen Time," *Business Insider*, March 4, 2020, https://www.businessinsider.co.za/tech-execs-screen-time-children-bill-gates-steve-jobs-2019-9.
5. National Day of Unplugging, https://www.nationaldayofunplugging.com/.
6. John Doerr, *Measure What Matters: How Google, Bono, and the Gates Foundation Rock the World with OKRs* (New York: Penguin Publishing Group, 2018), 56.
7. John Piper, *Desiring God: Meditations of a Christian Hedonist,* 2nd ed. (Portland, OR: Multnomah Press, 1996), 50.

Chapter 10 – Resolution #7: Redeem Time

1. William Penn, *Passages from the Life and Writings of William Penn* (United States, For Sale at Friend's book-store, 1882), 384.
2. Felix Richter, "Always On: Media Usage Amounts to 10+ Hours a Day," *Statista*, January 16, 2019, https://www.statista.com/chart/1971/electronic-media-use/.
3. Roland Sturm and Deborah A. Cohen, "Free Time and Physical Activity Among Americans 15 Years or Older: Cross-Sectional Analysis of the American Time Use Survey," Centers for Disease Control and Prevention, September 26, 2019, https://www.cdc.gov/pcd/issues/2019/19_0017.htm.

4. Charles H. Spurgeon, *The Treasury of David*, vol. 4 (New York: Funk & Wagnalls, 1882), 203, emphasis added.
5. Danielle Pacheco, "Sleep Satisfaction and Energy Levels," Sleep Foundation, updated January 8, 2021, https://www.sleepfoundation.org/sleep-hygiene/sleep-satisfaction-and-energy-levels.
6. Logan Foley, "Why Do We Need Sleep?," Sleep Foundation, updated September 11, 2020, https://www.sleepfoundation.org/how-sleep-works/why-do-we-need-sleep.
7. Ibid.
8. Gordon MacDonald, *Ordering Your Private World* (Nashville, TN: Thomas Nelson, 2003), 110–17.